Oil Painting N Colored Pencil Inspiration Book

Colored Pencil Books N Oil Painting Ideas for Beginners

By Priyank Gala

Published By:

Priyank Gala

ISBN-13: 978-1508629580
ISBN-10: 1508629587

©Copyright 2015 – Priyank Gala

OIL PAINTINGS

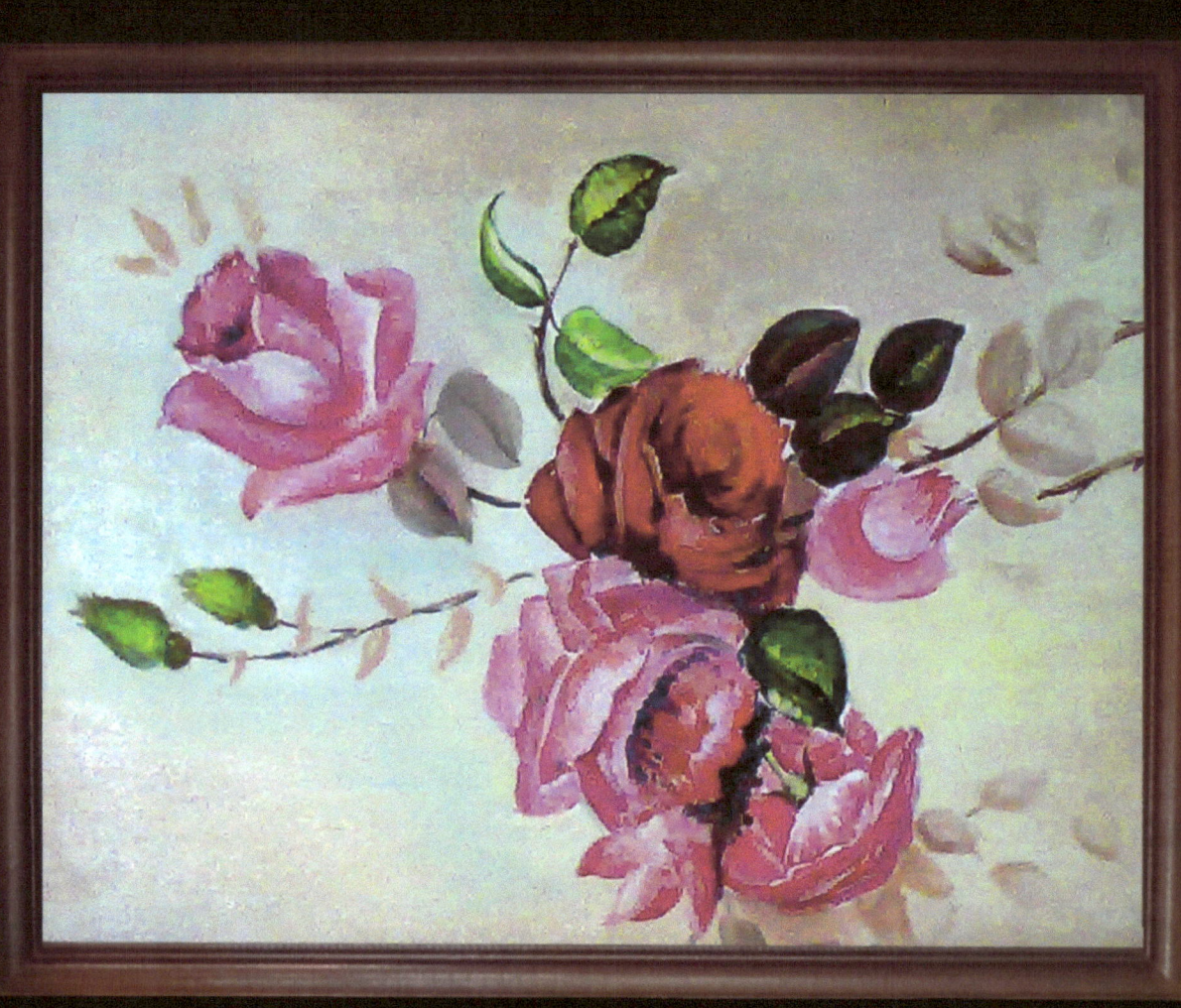

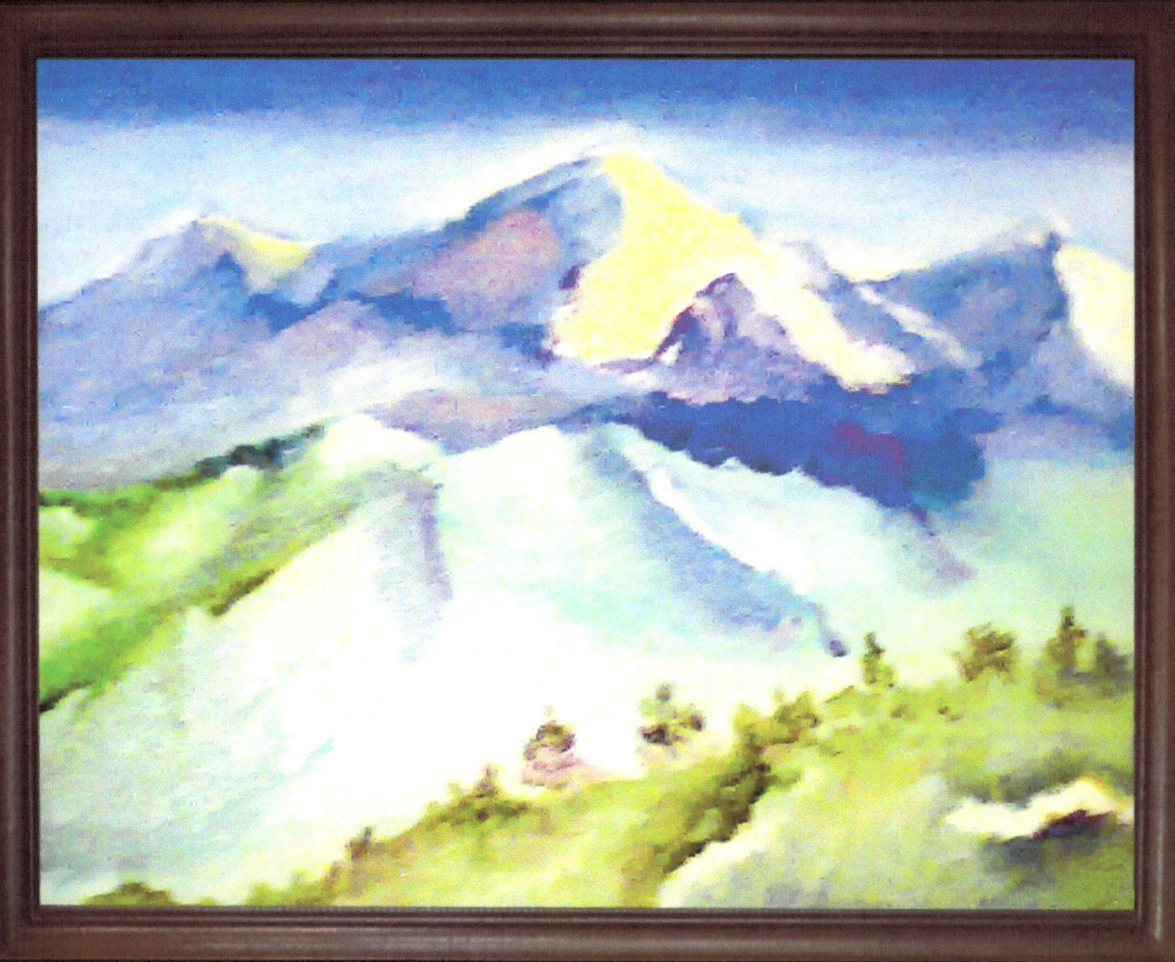

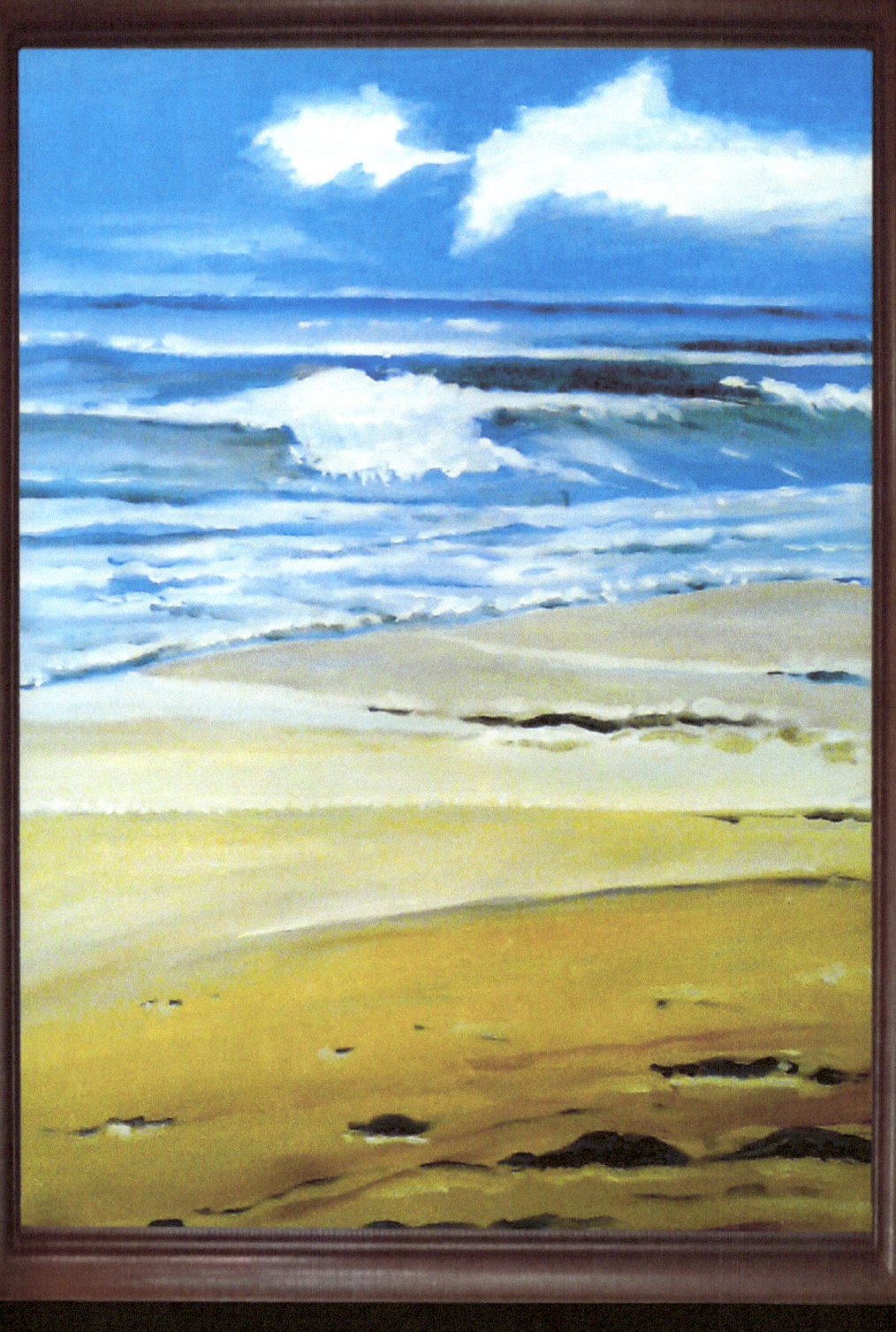

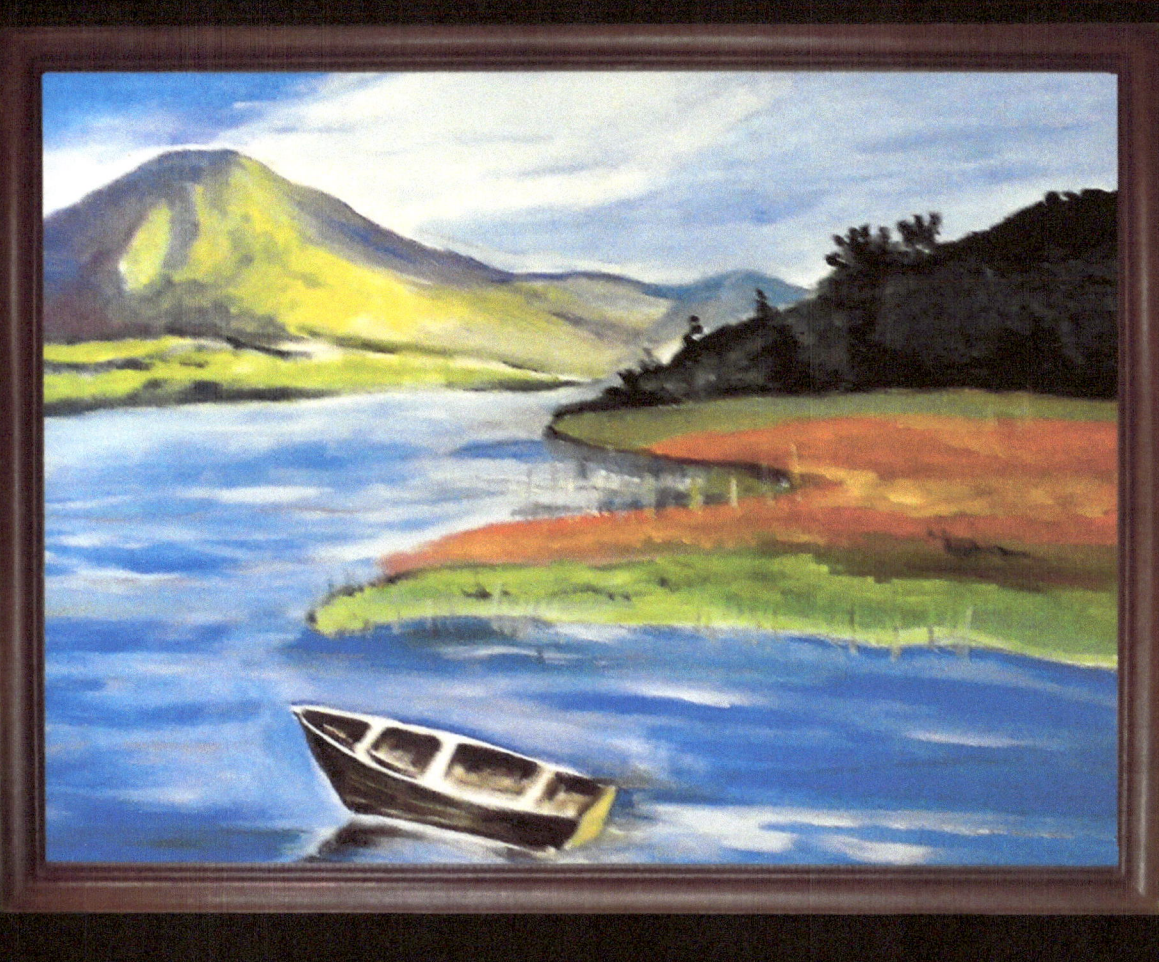

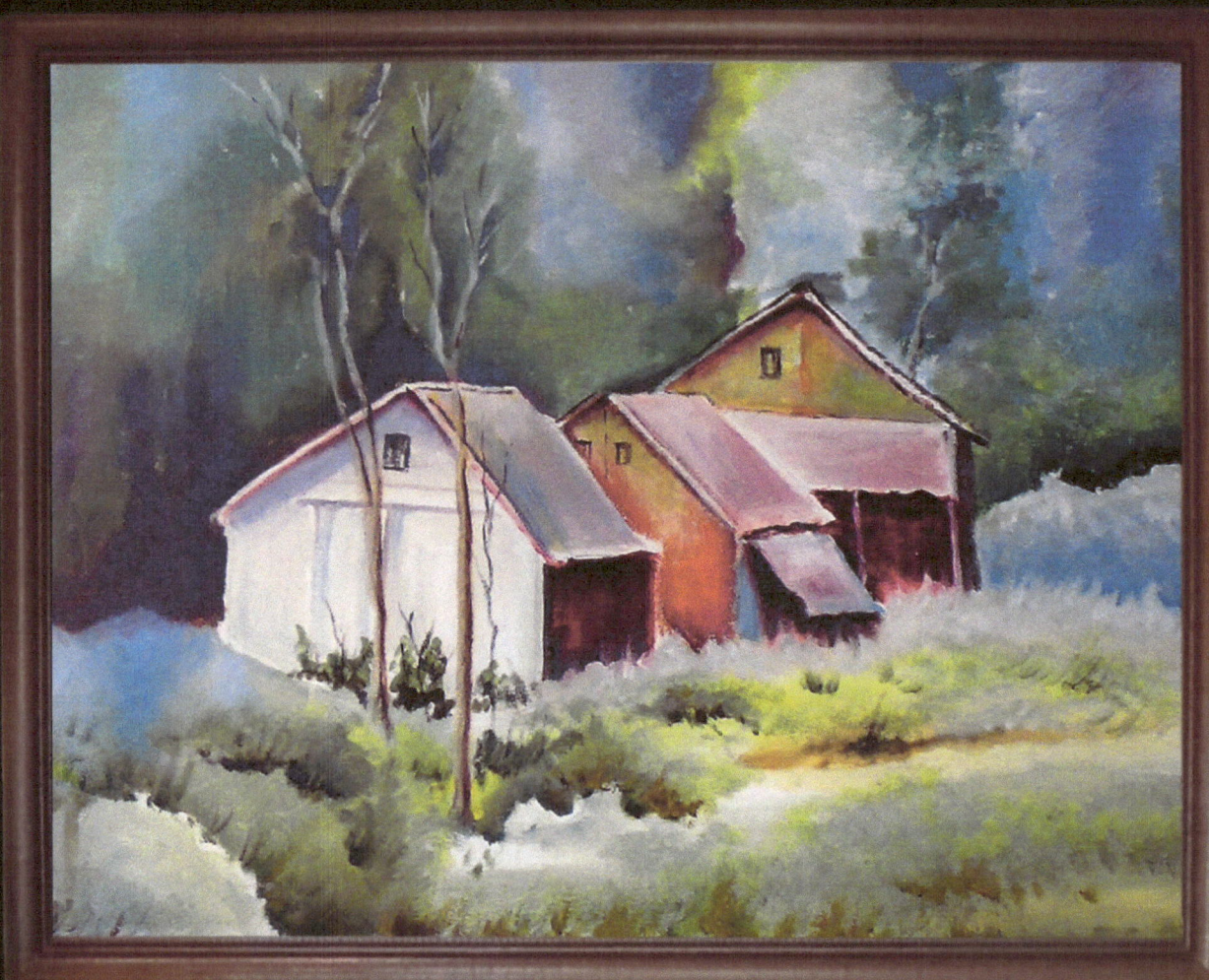

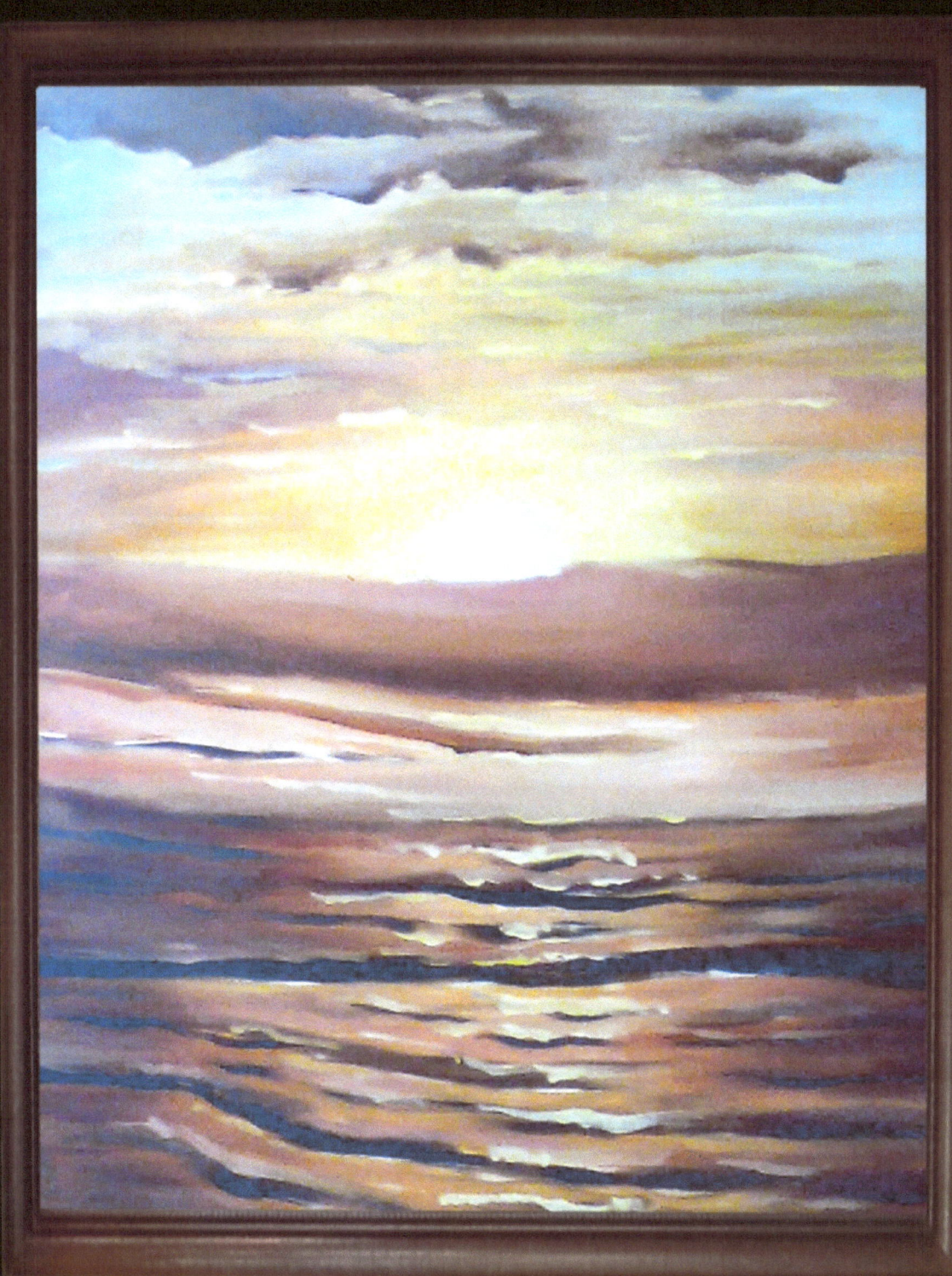

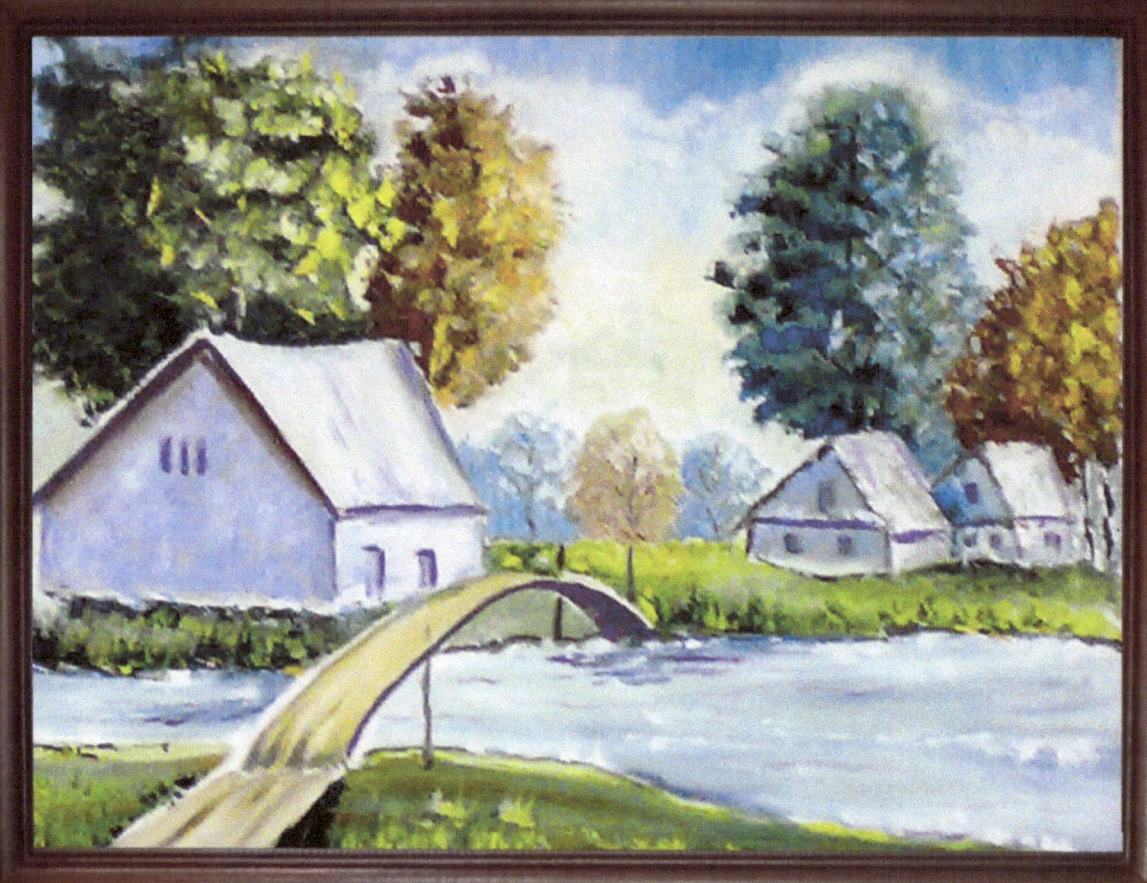

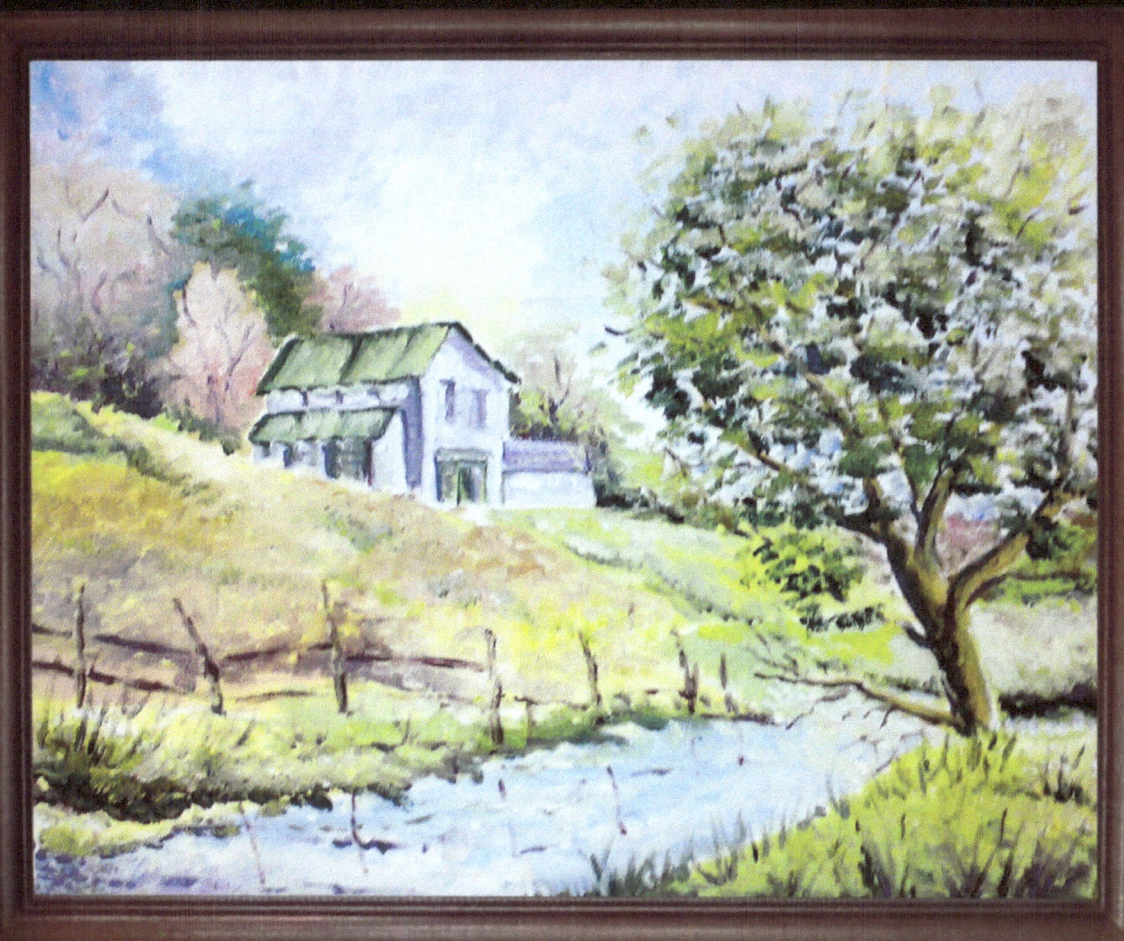

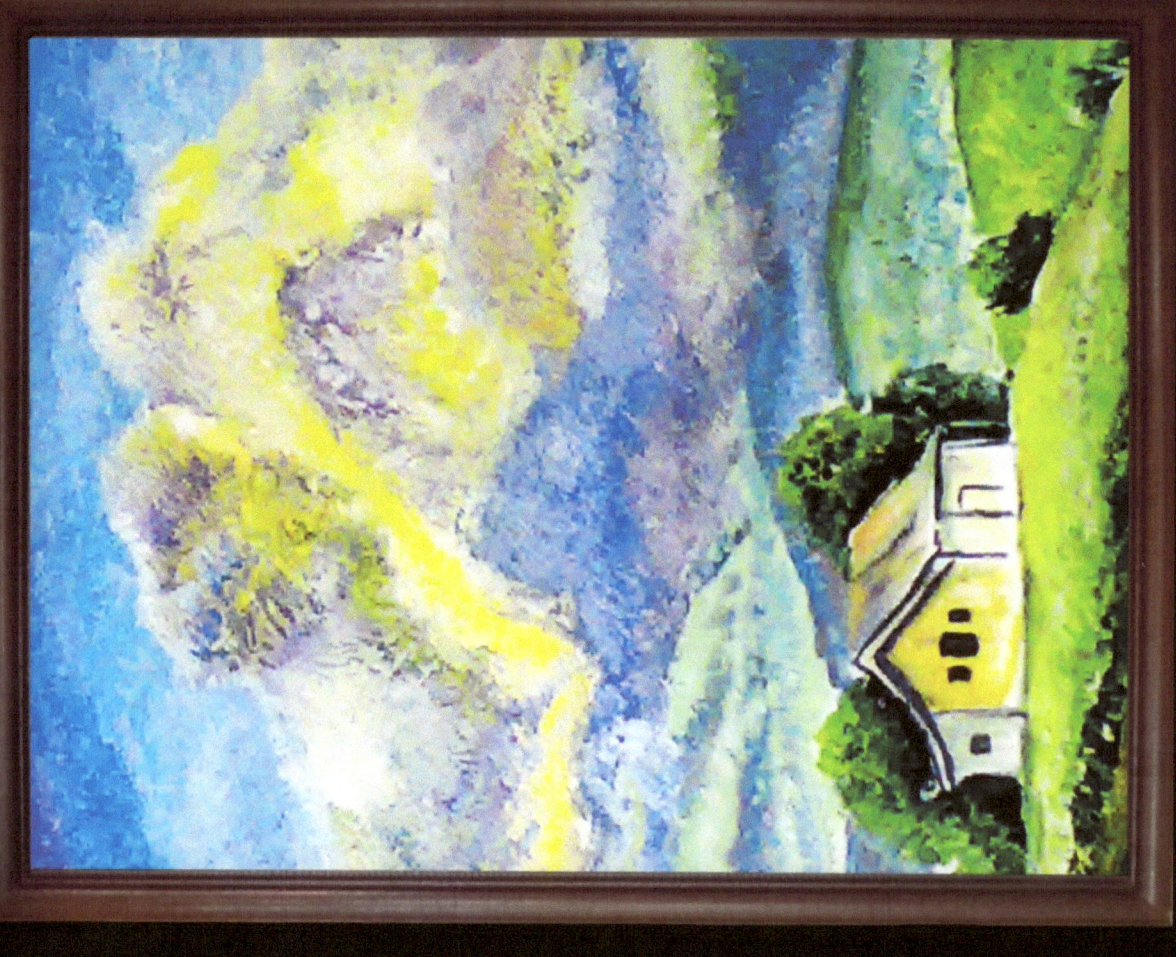

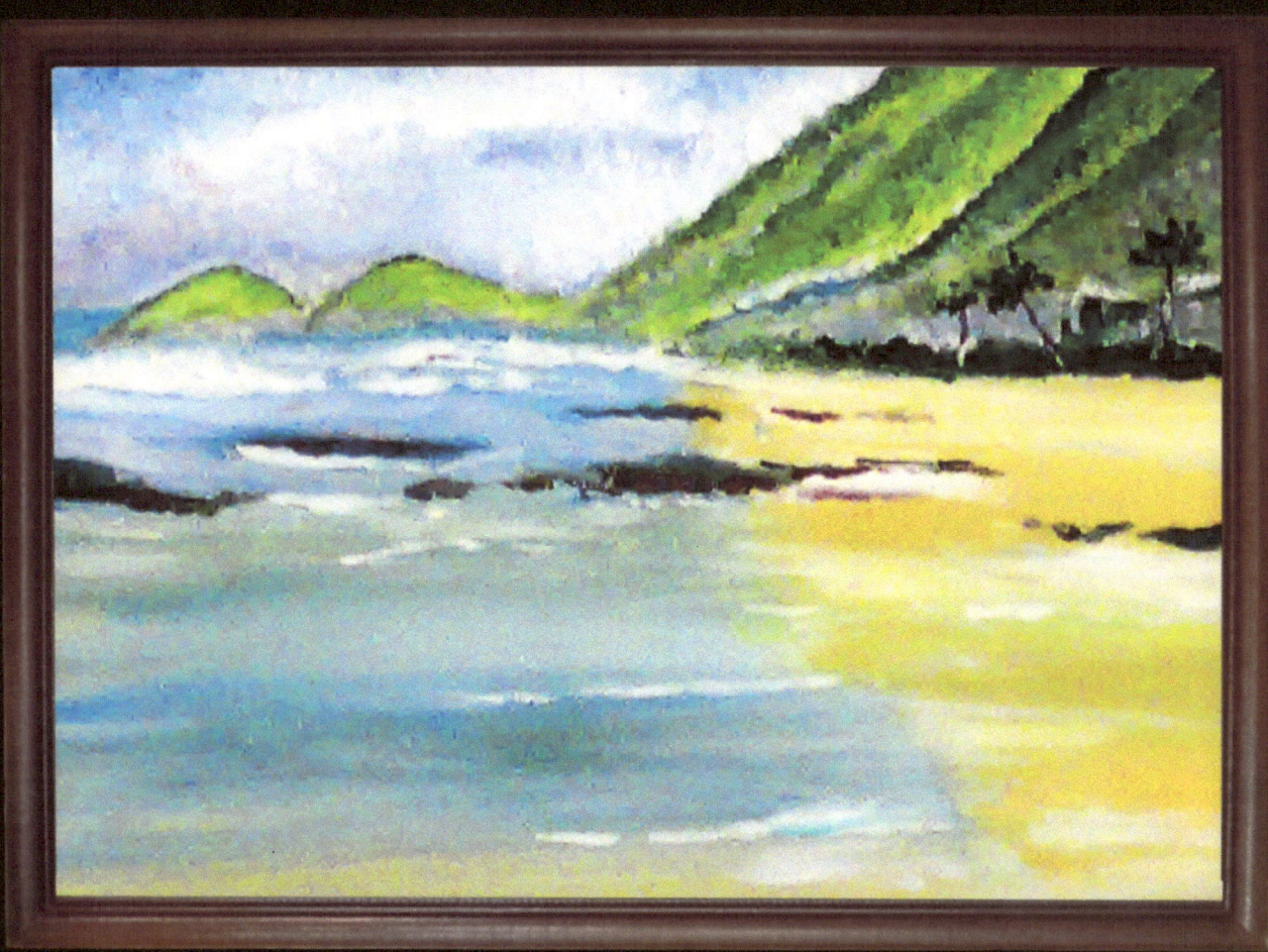

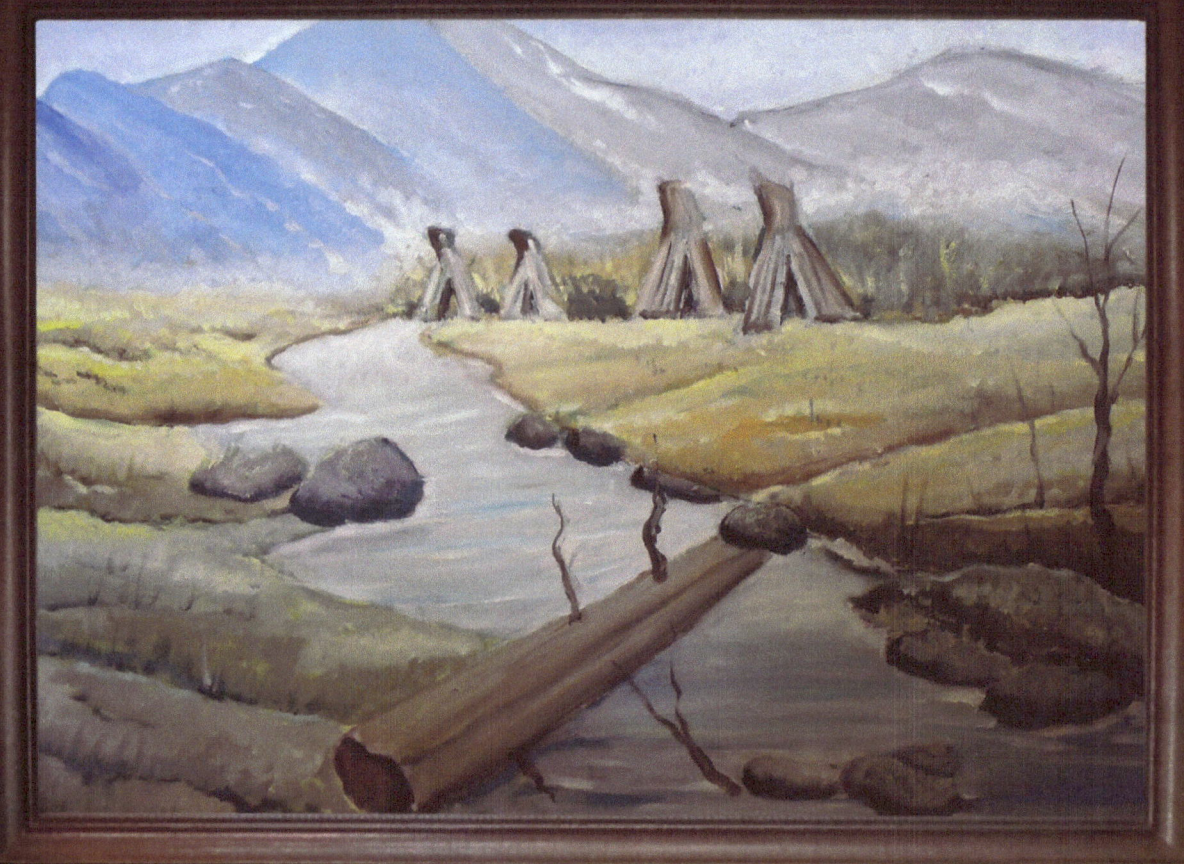

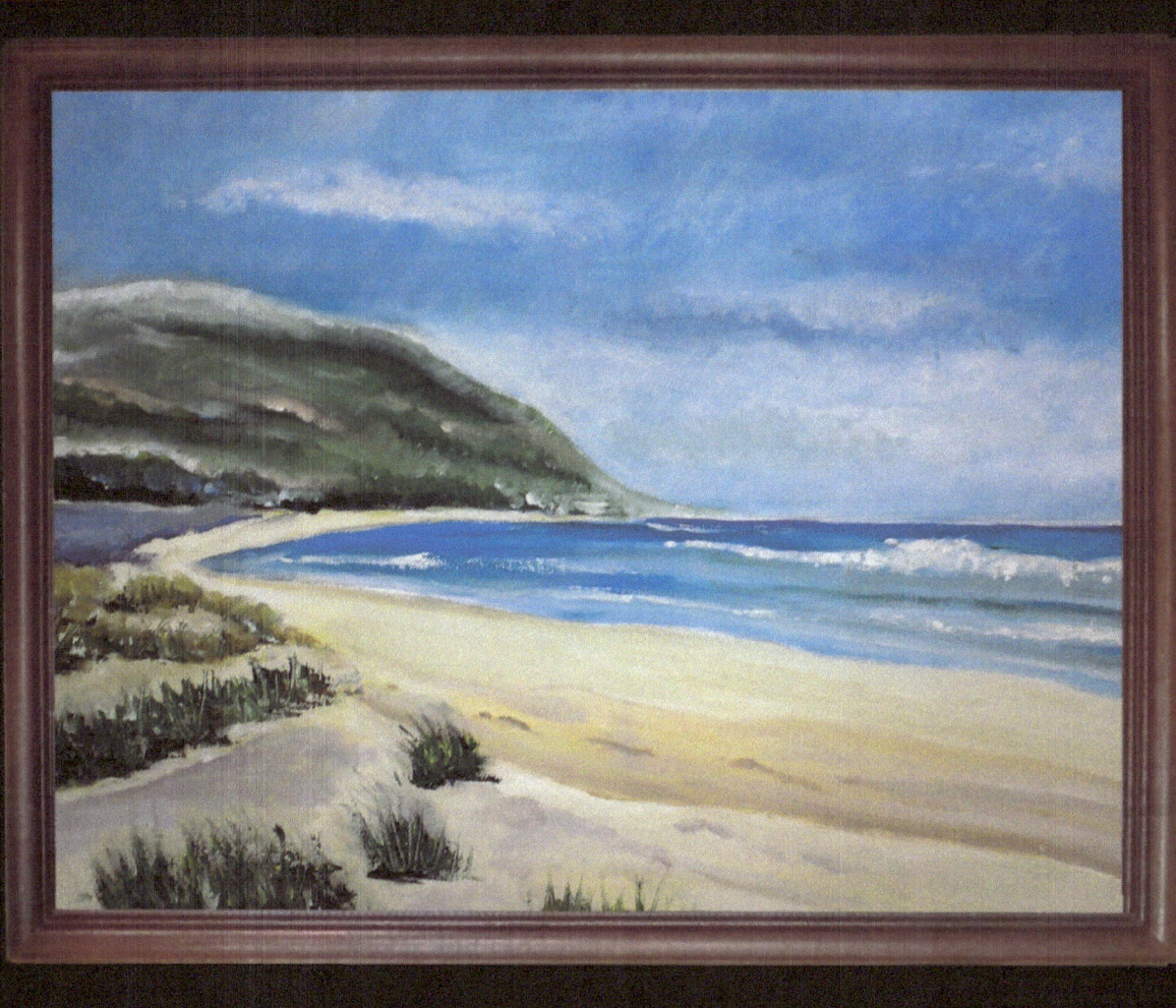

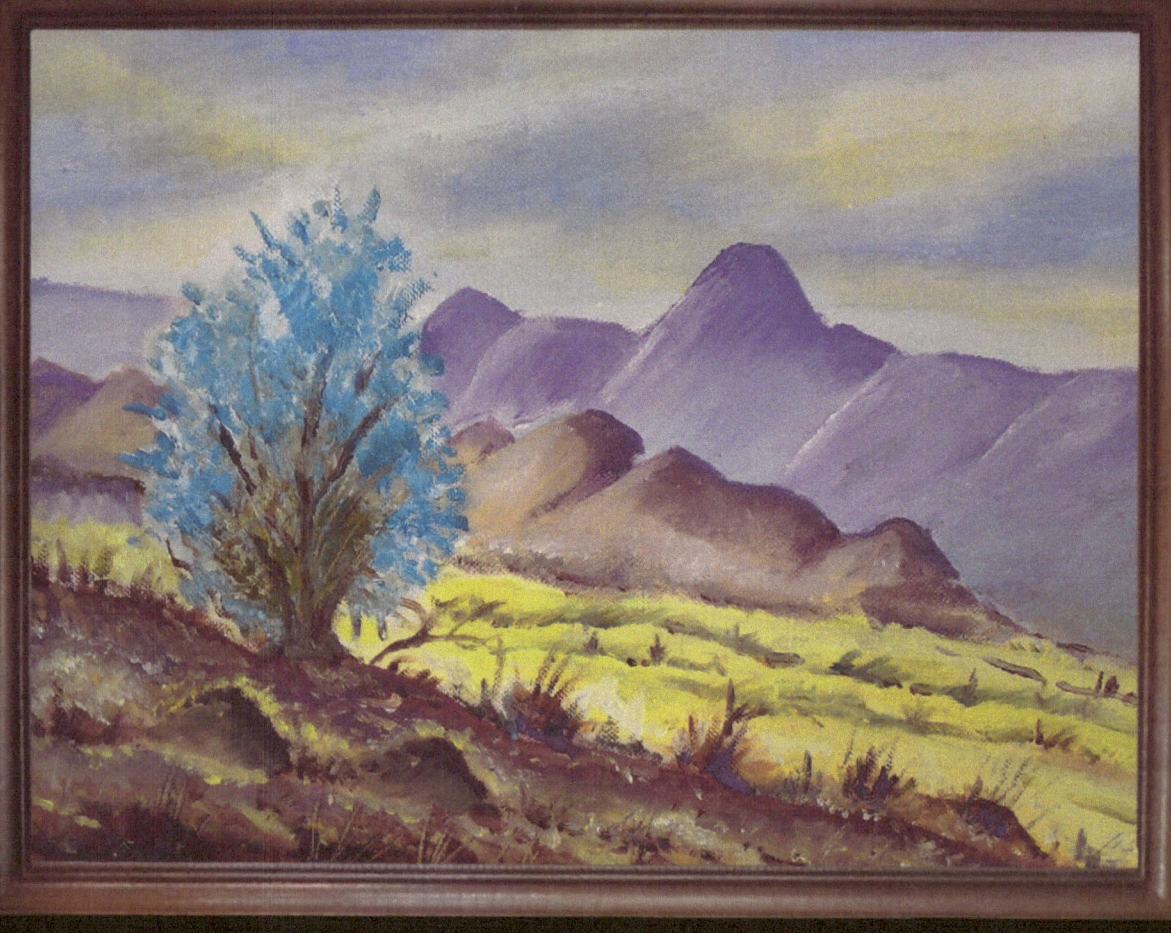

COLOR PENCIL

DRAWINGS

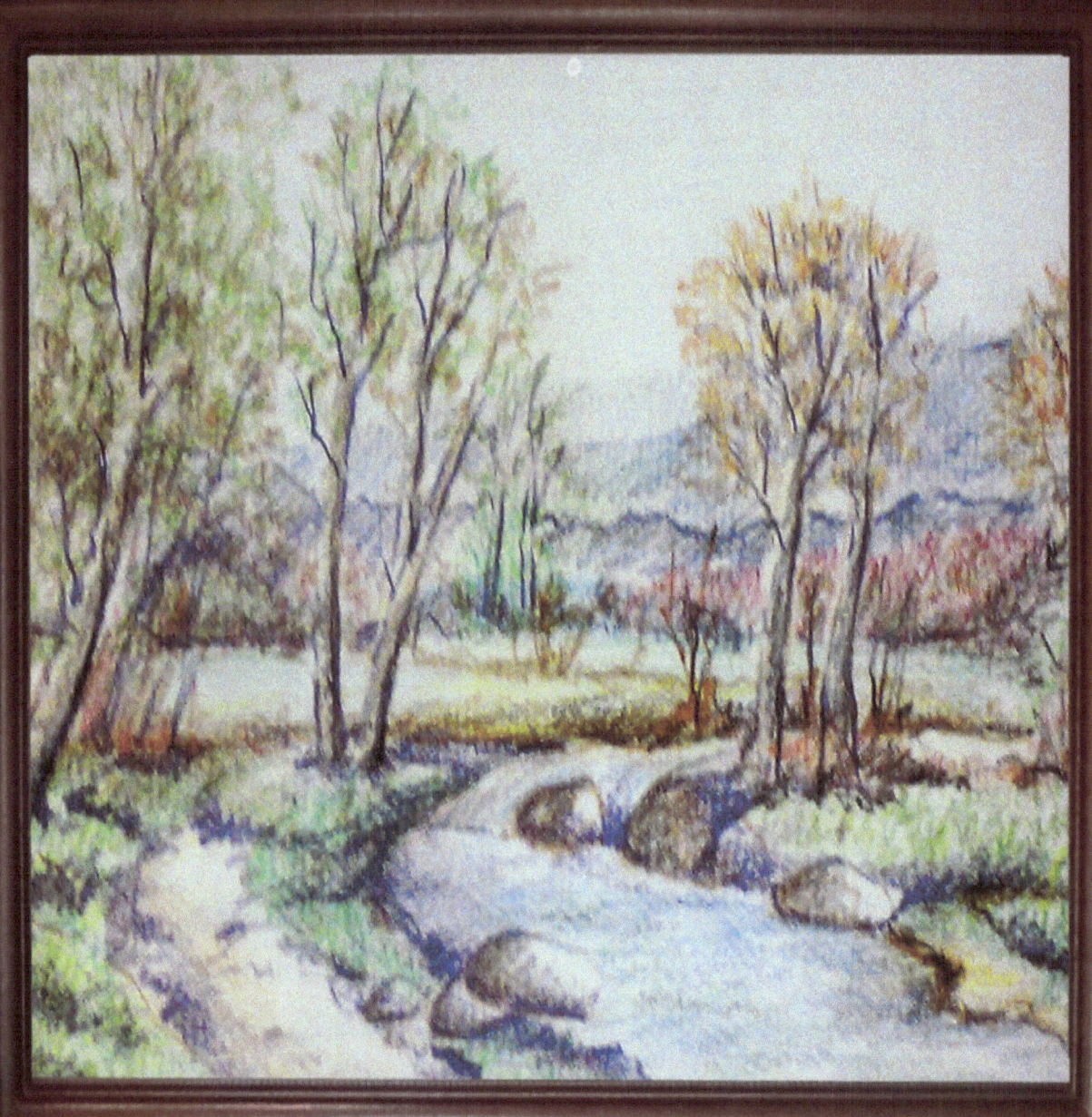

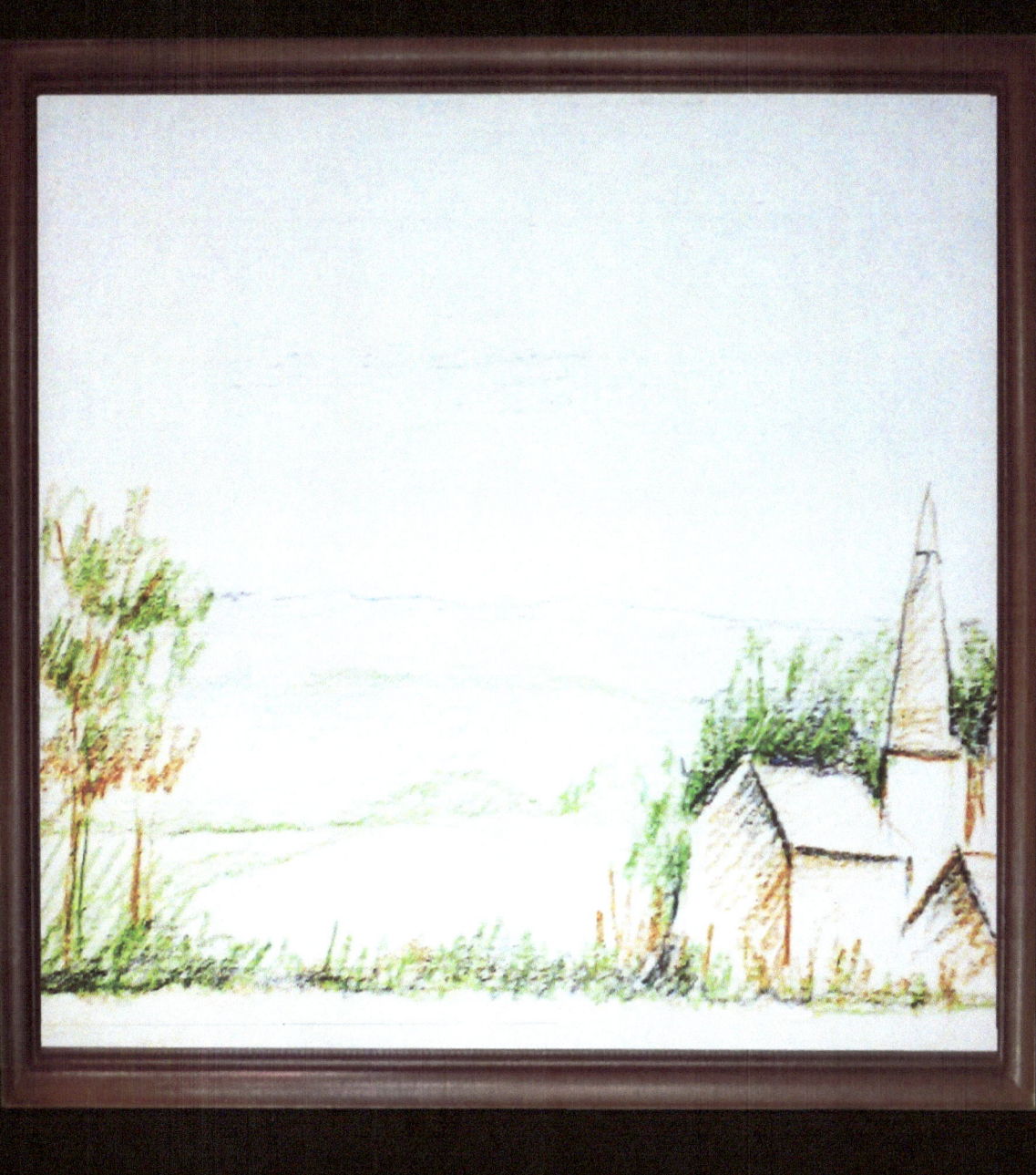

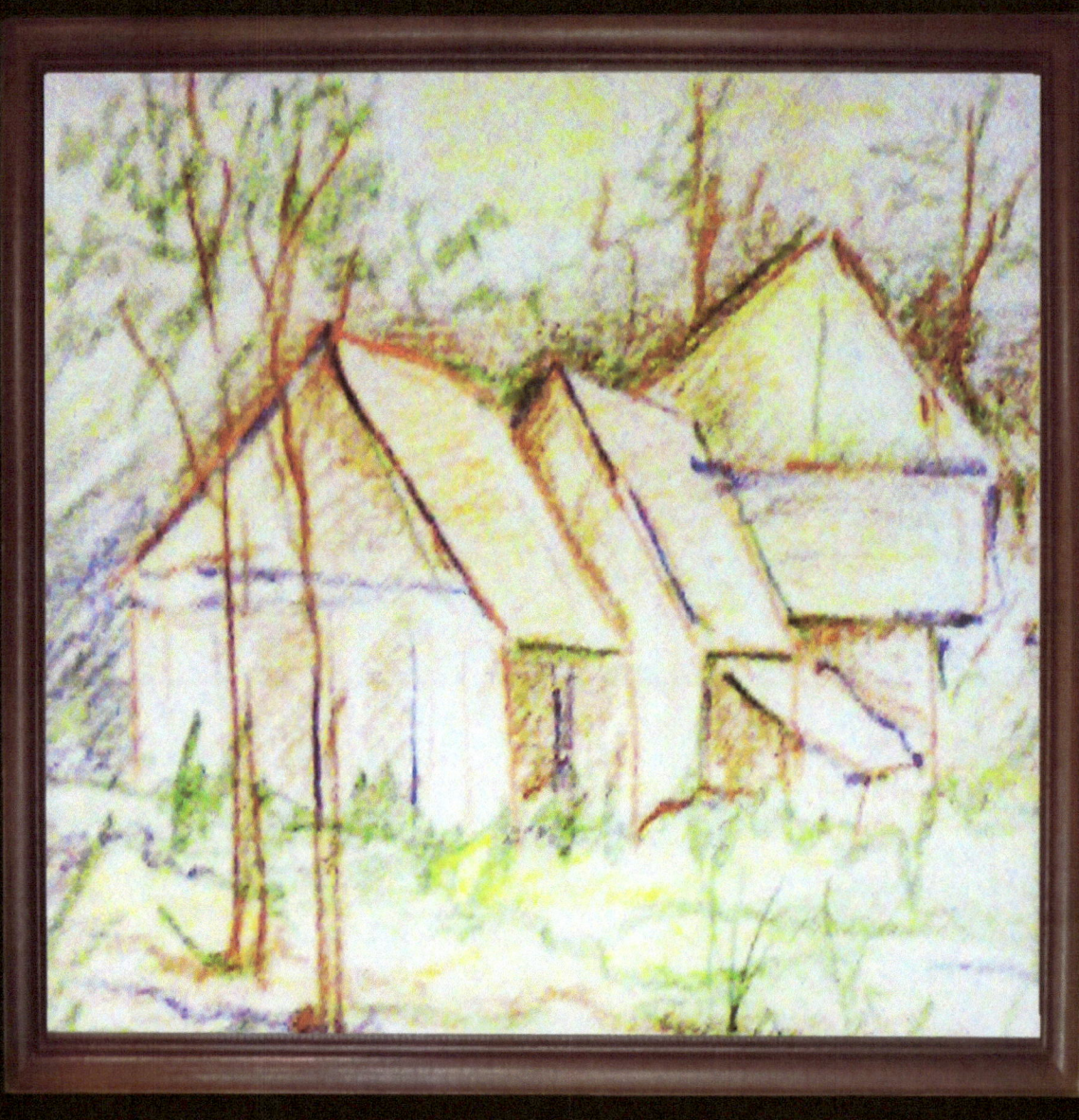

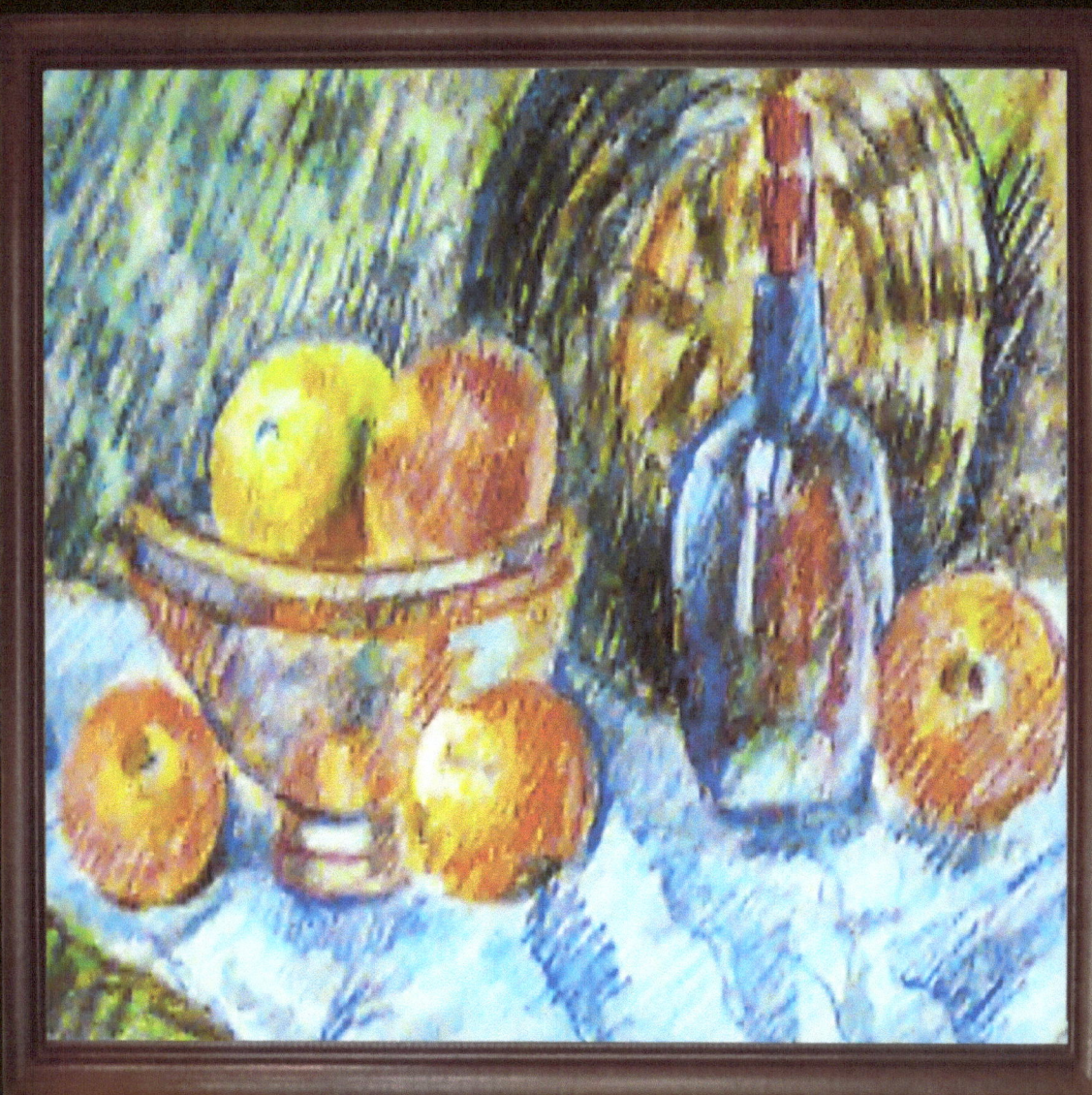

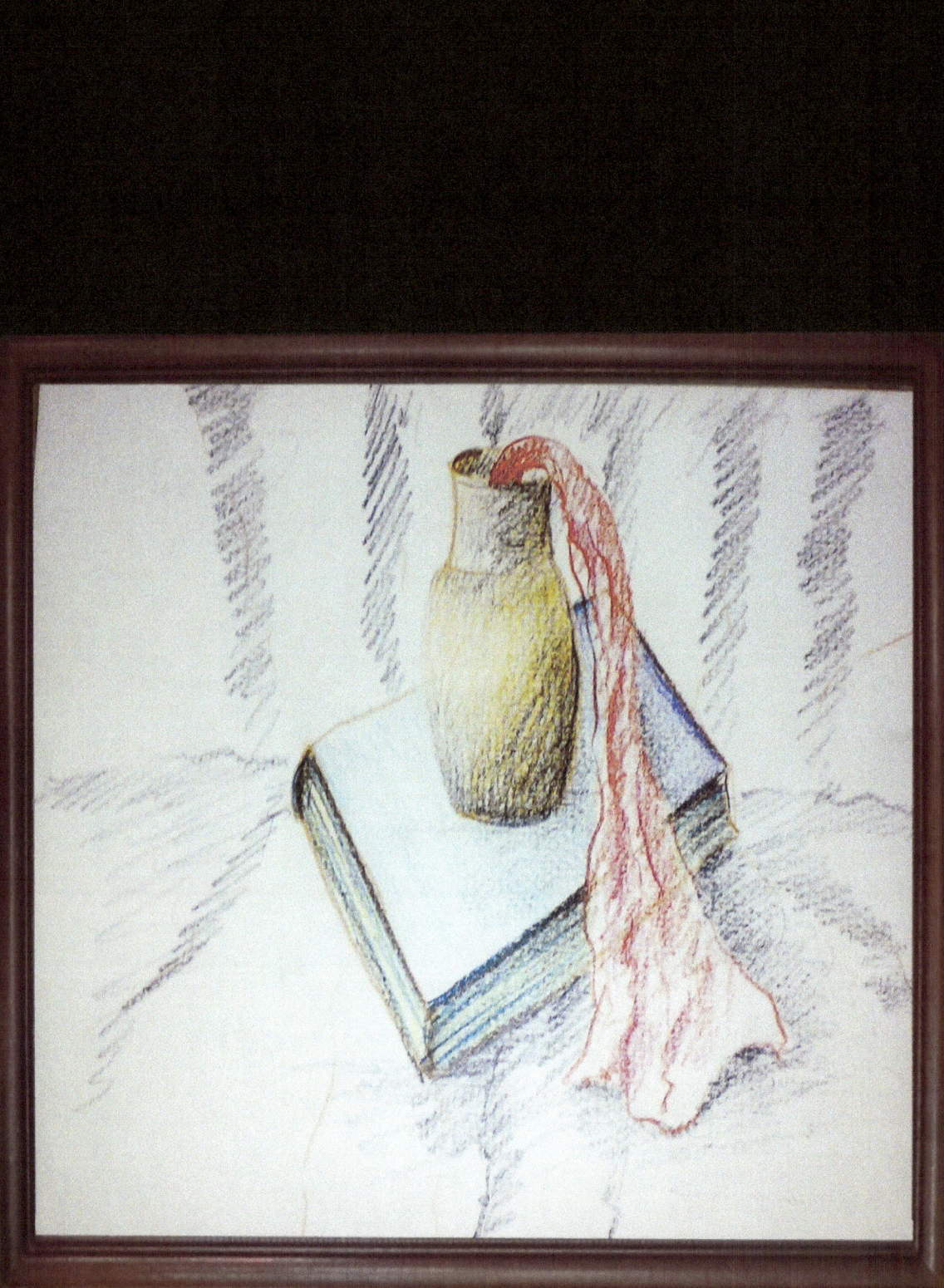

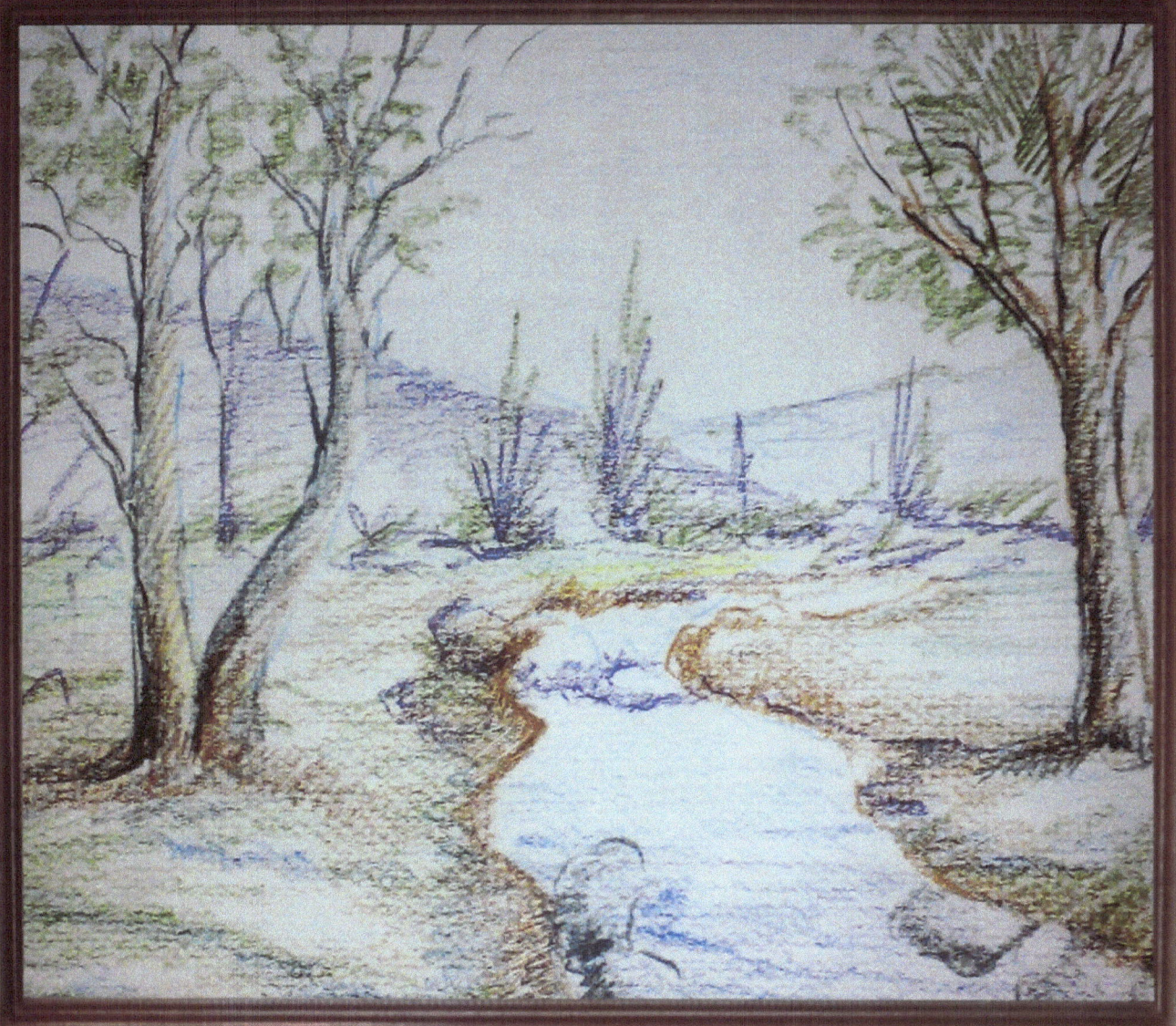

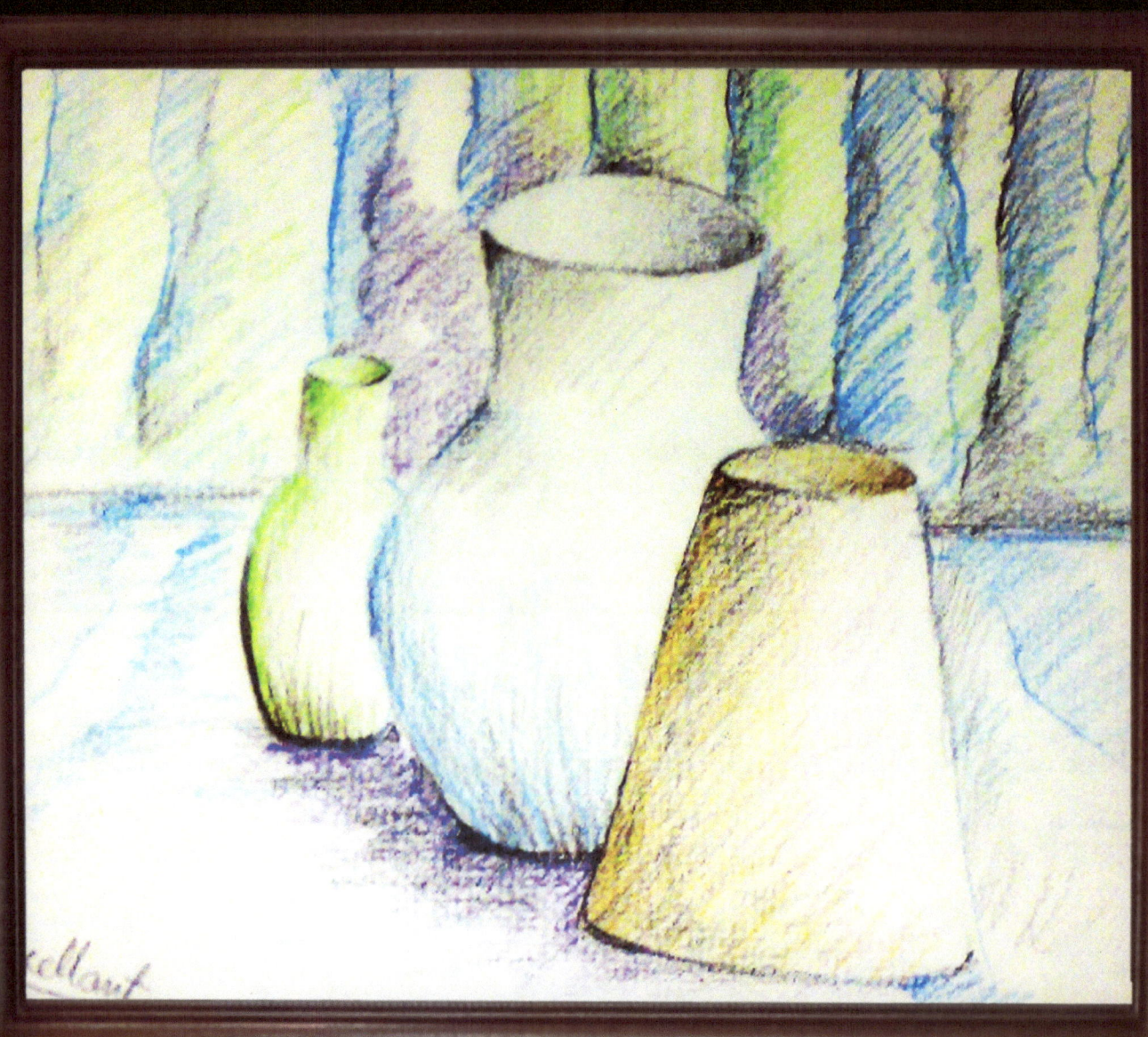

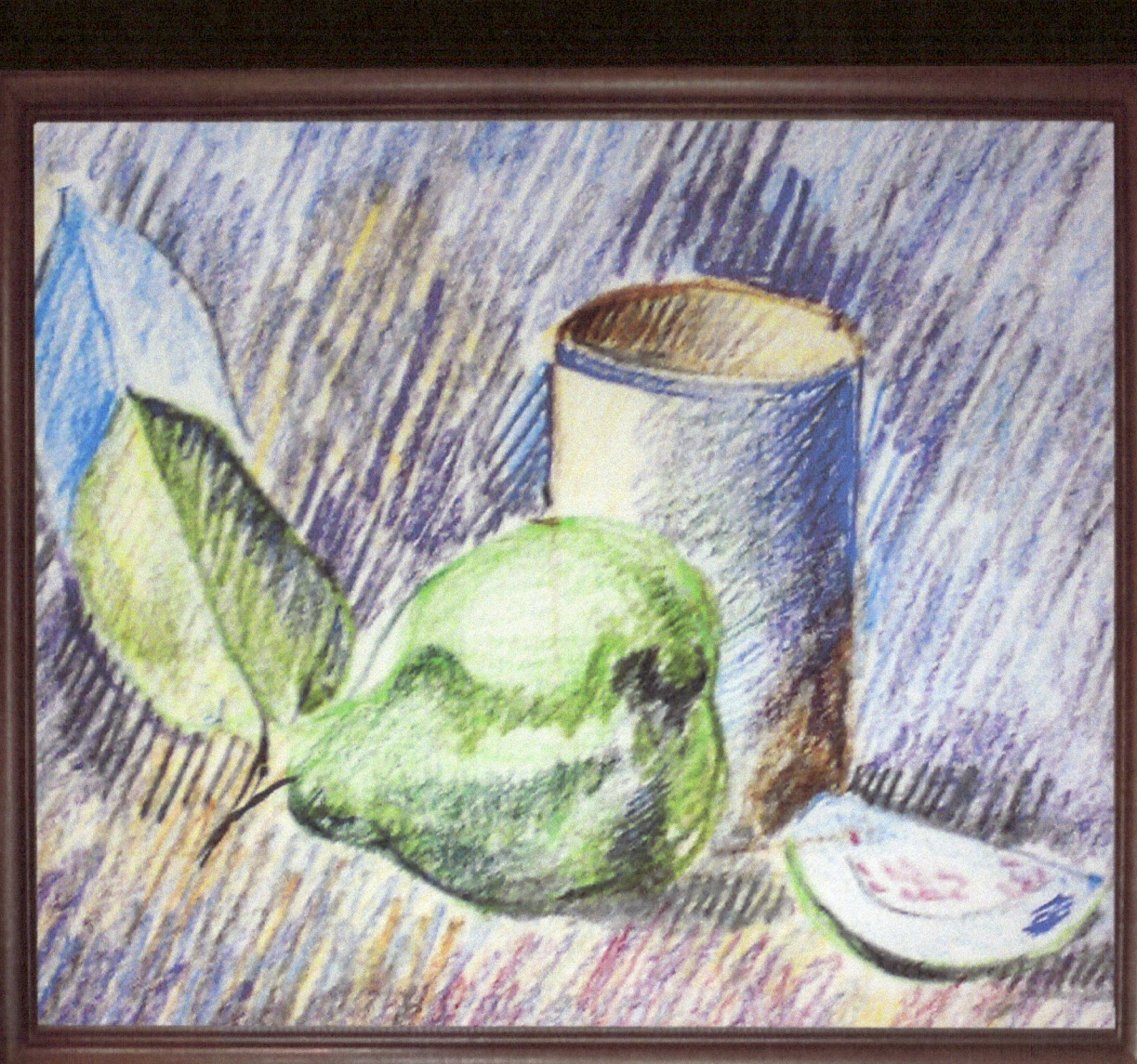

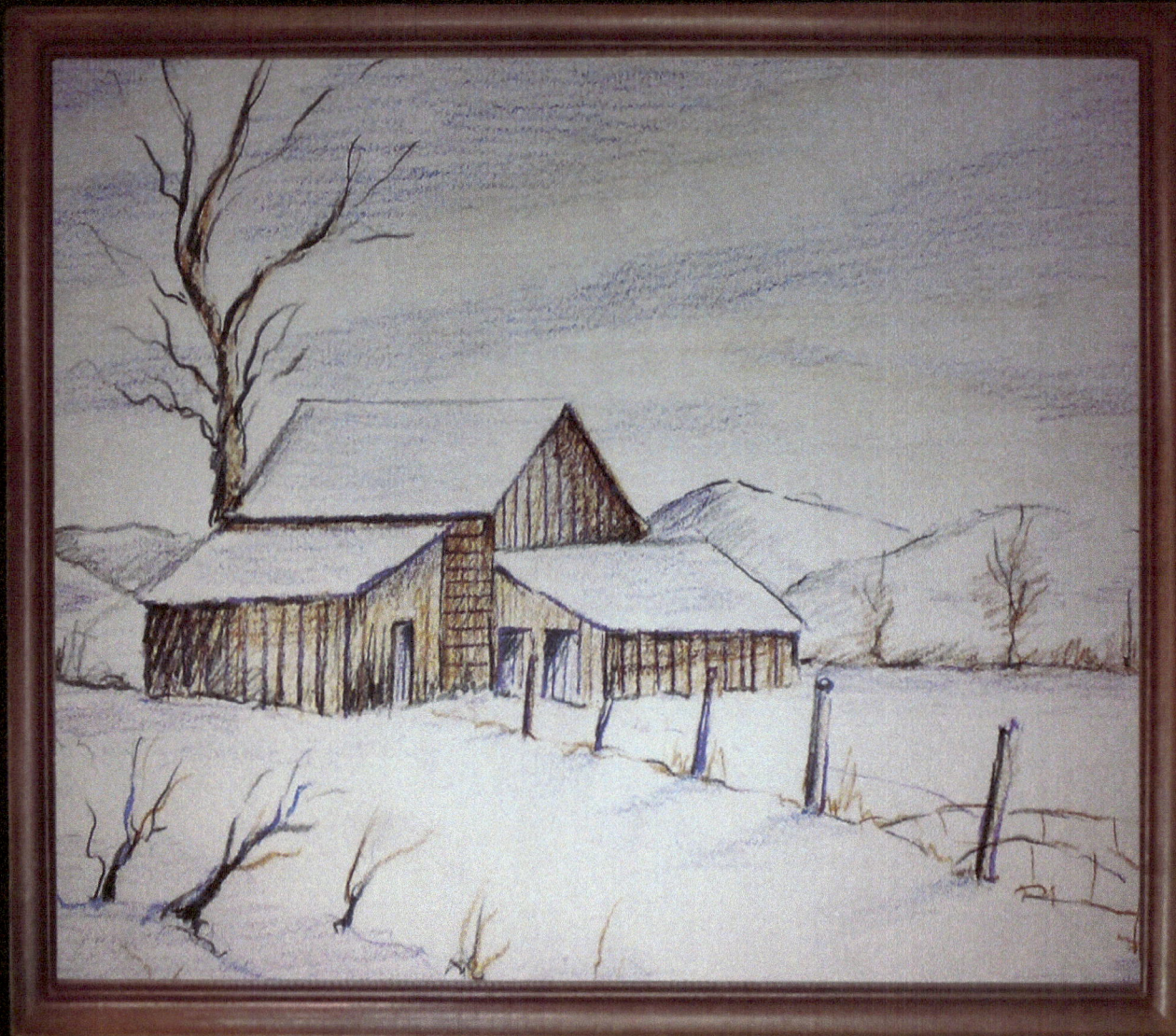

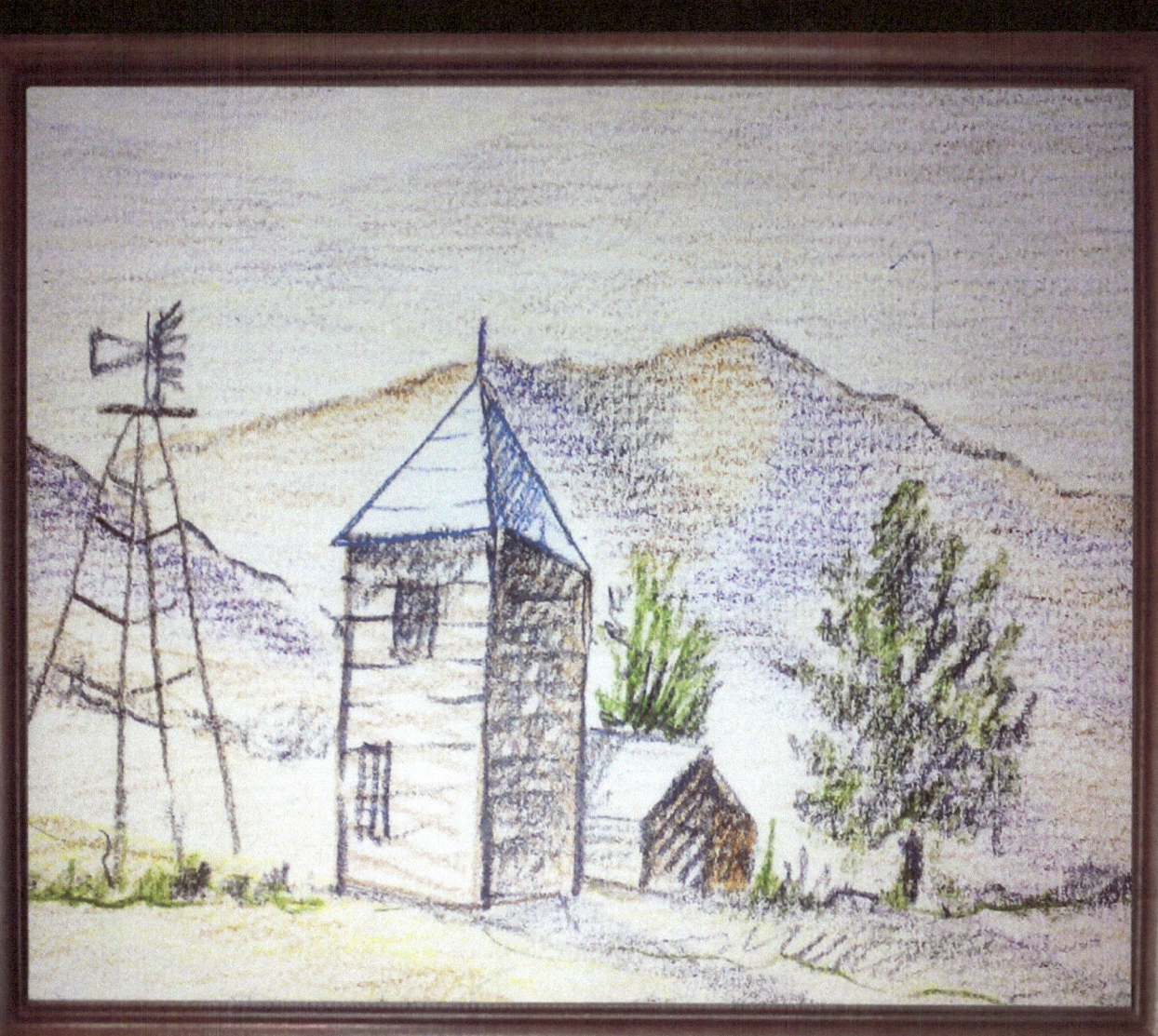

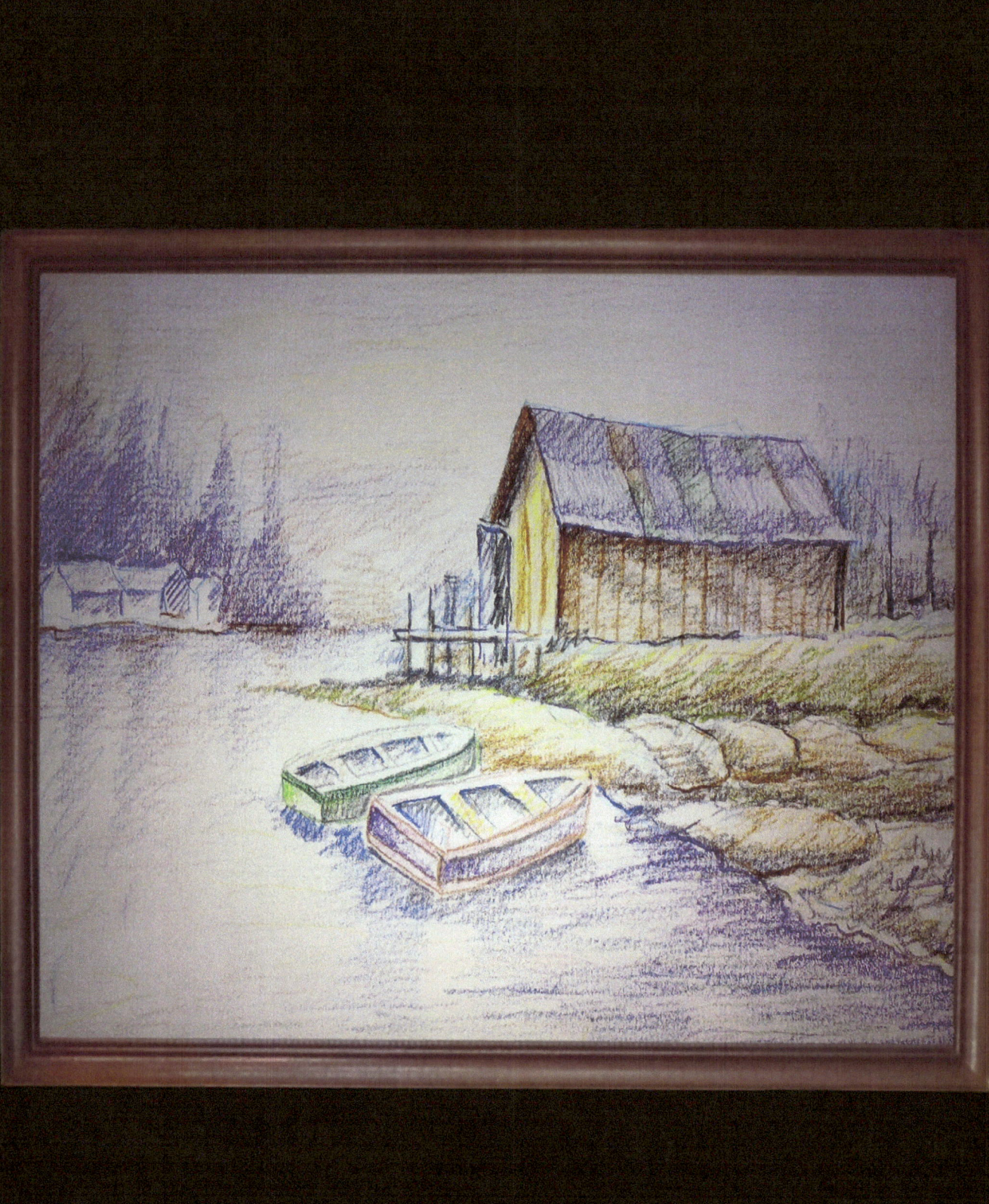

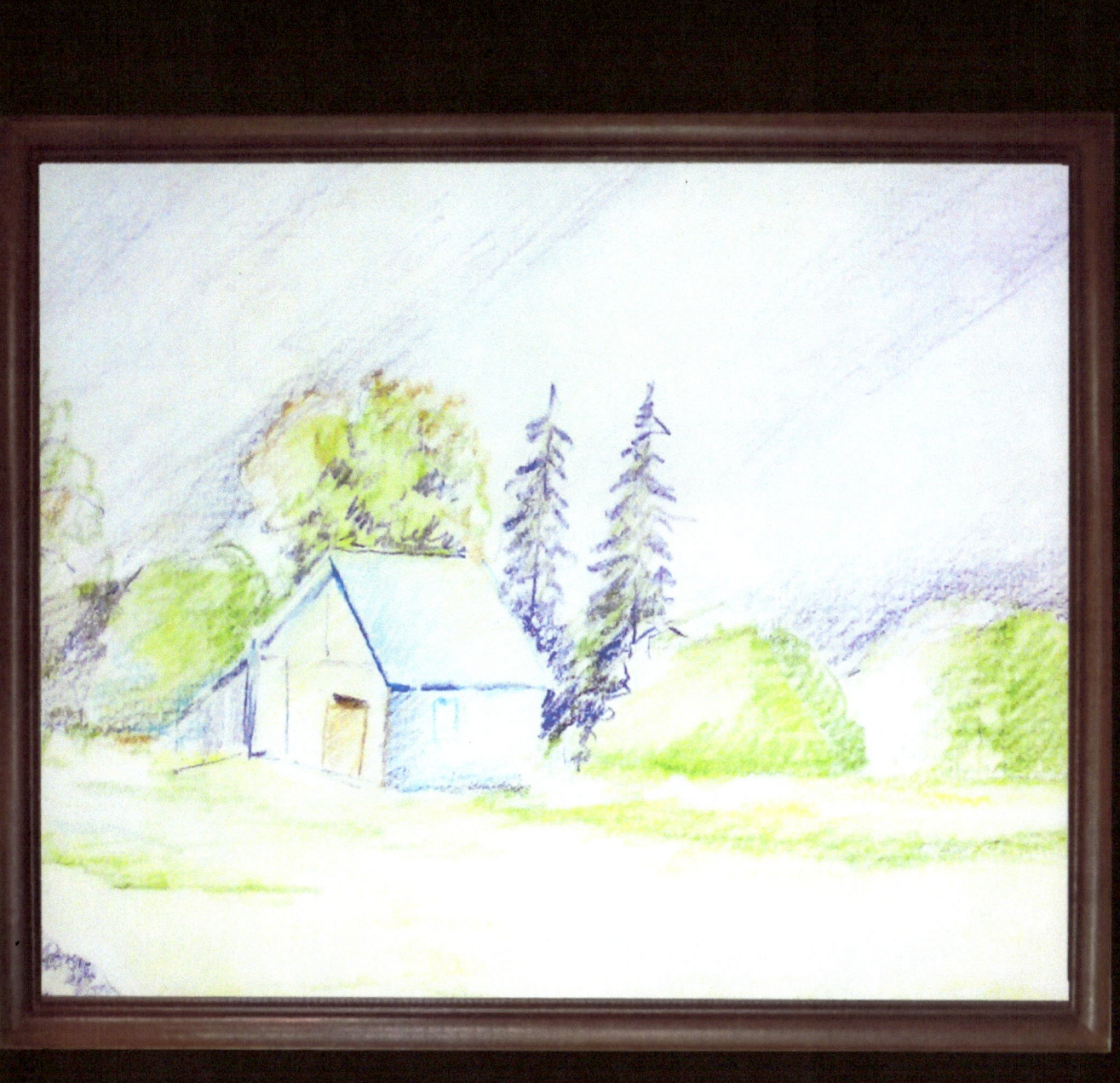

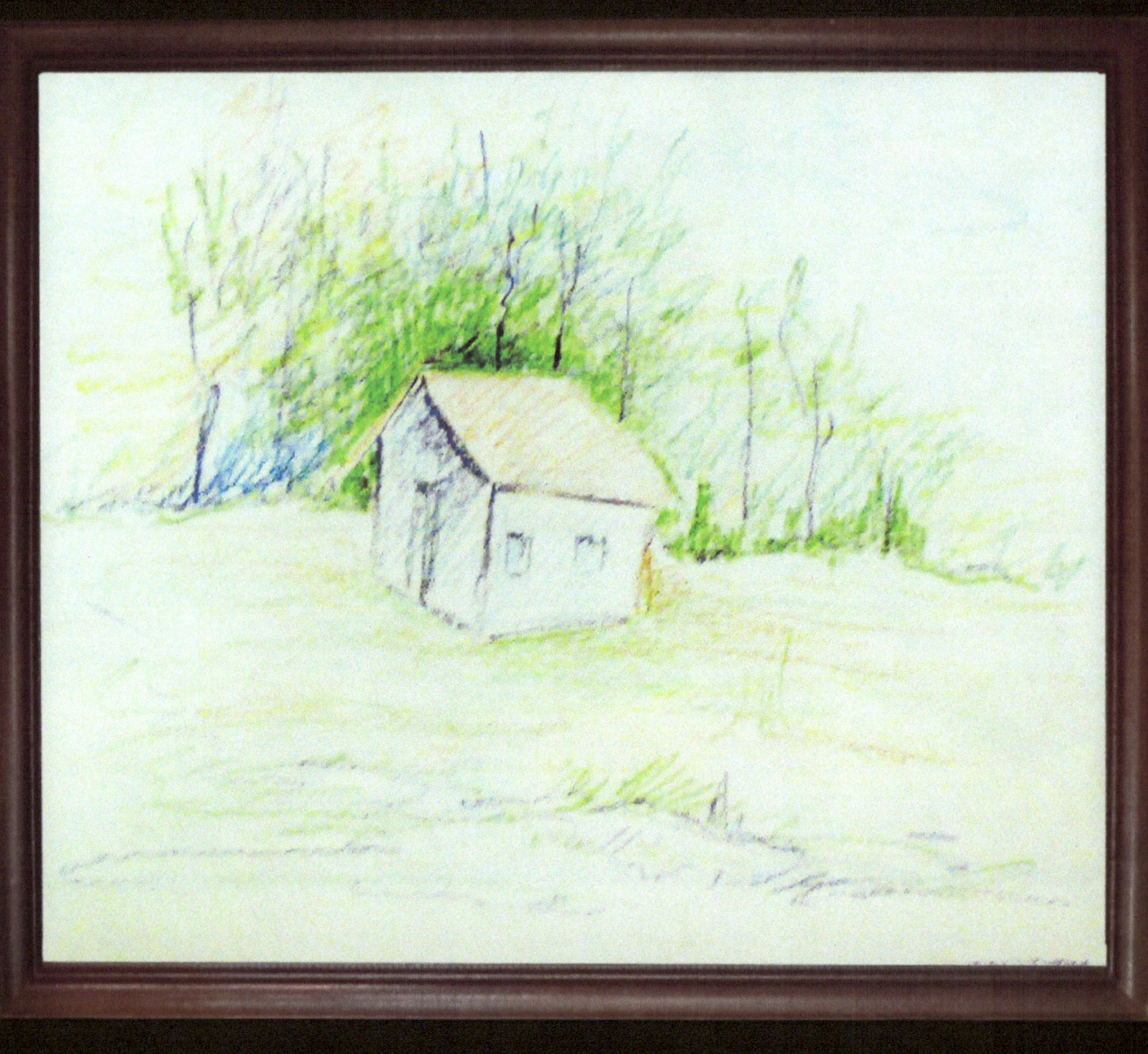

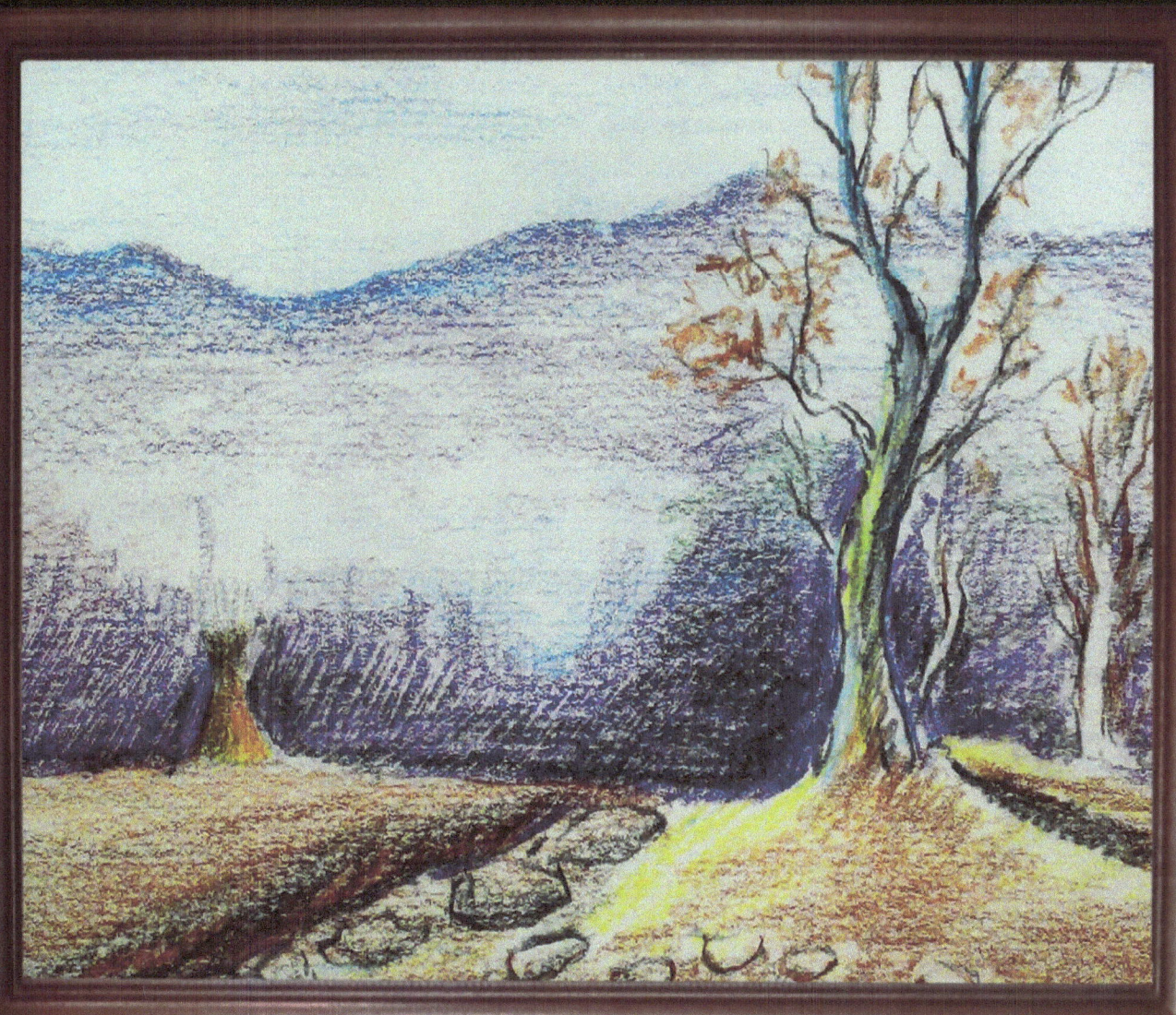

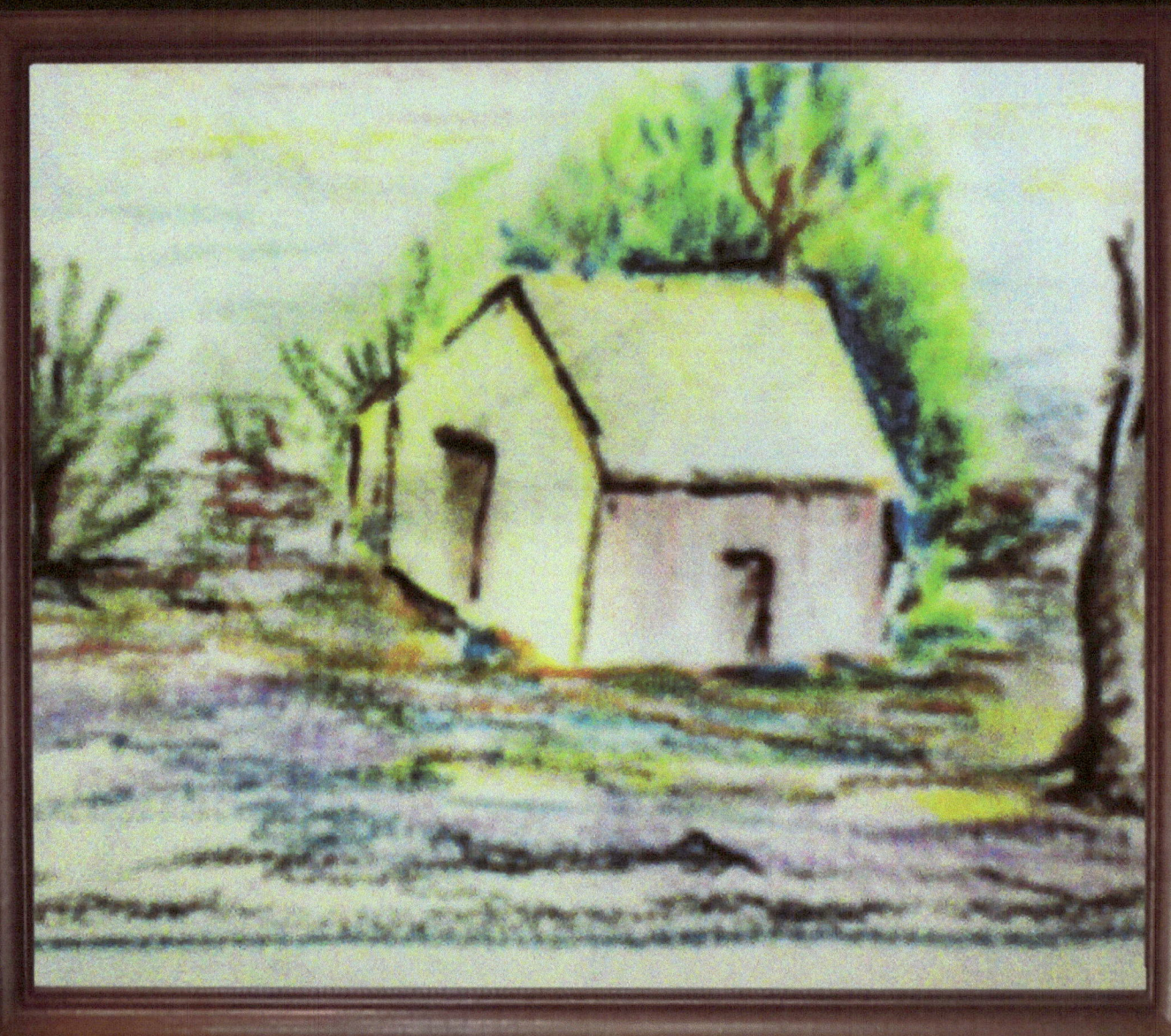

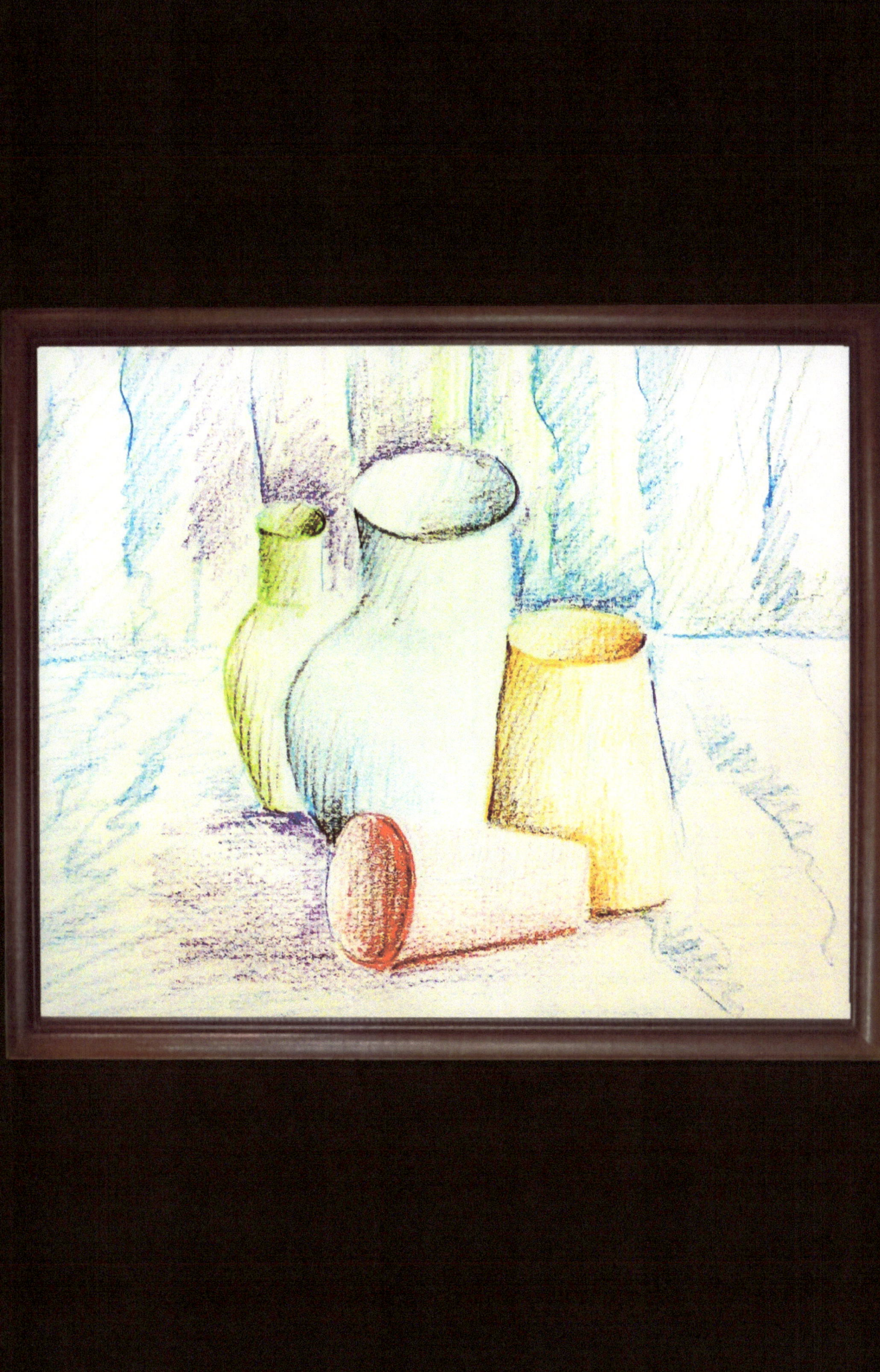

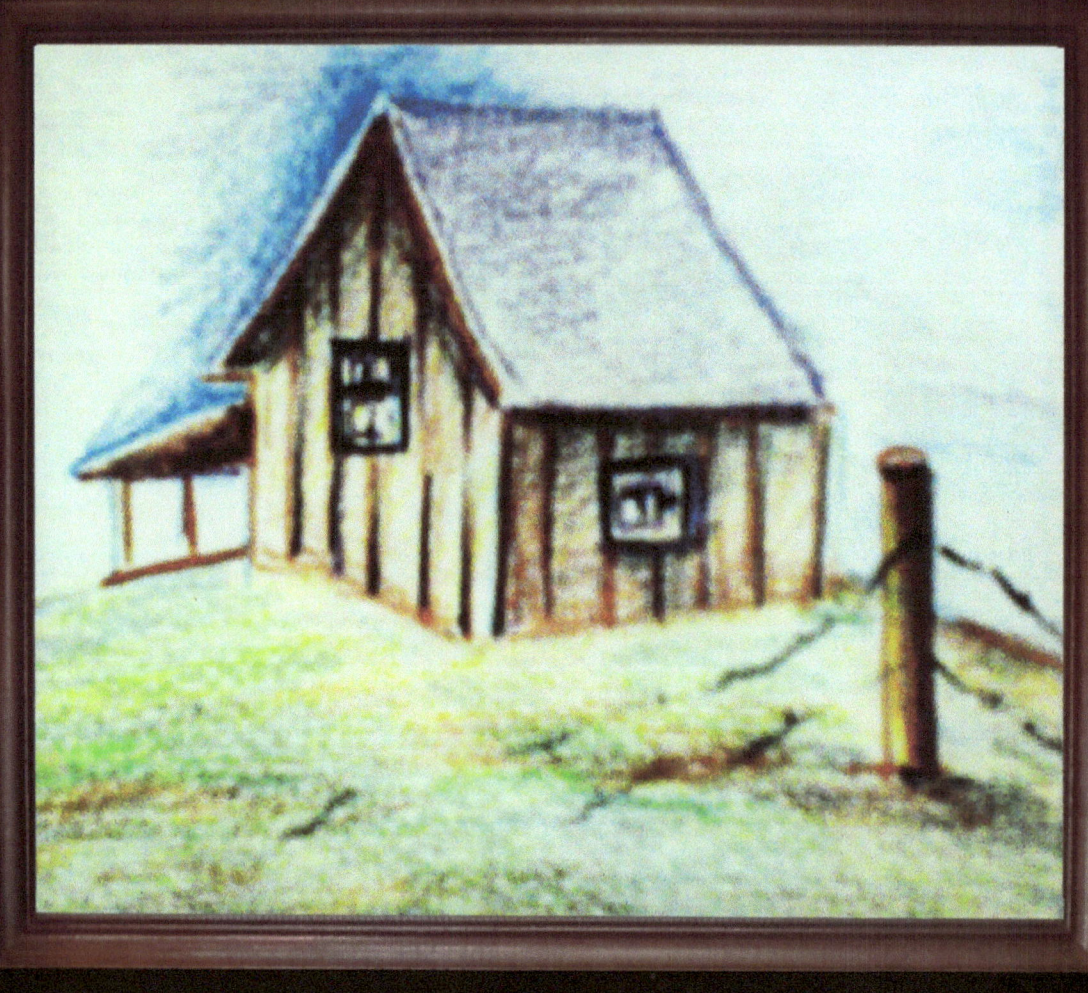

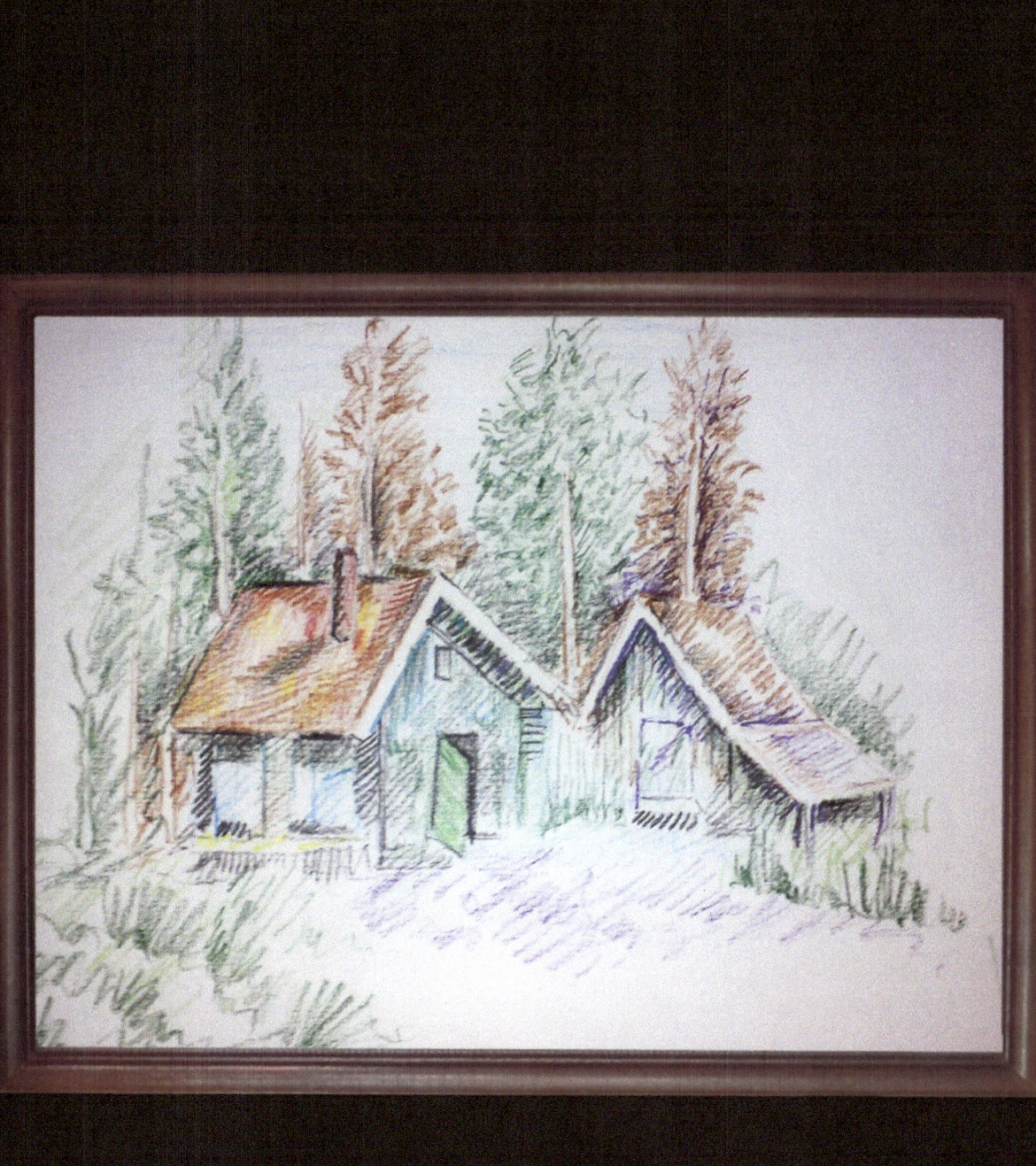

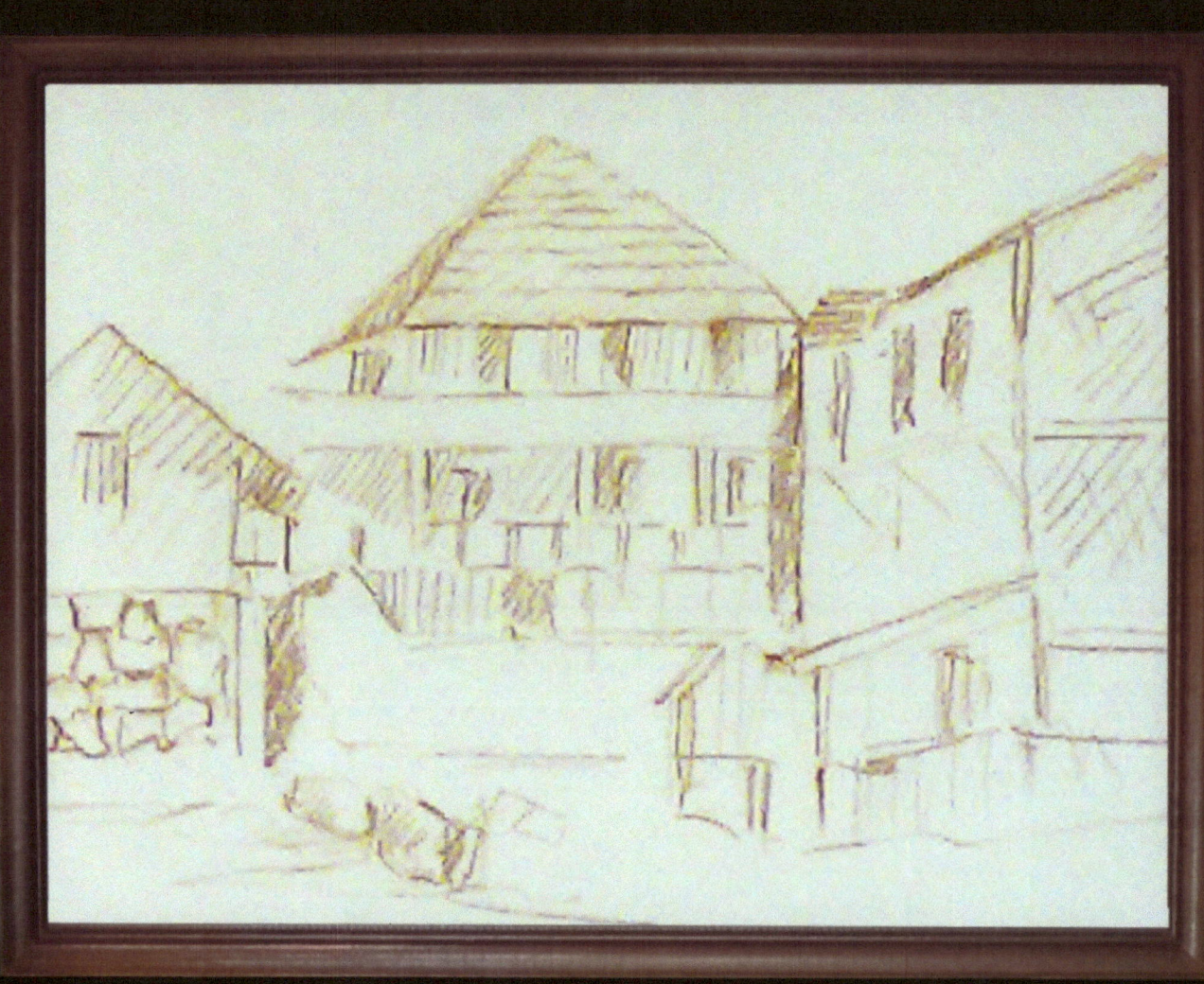

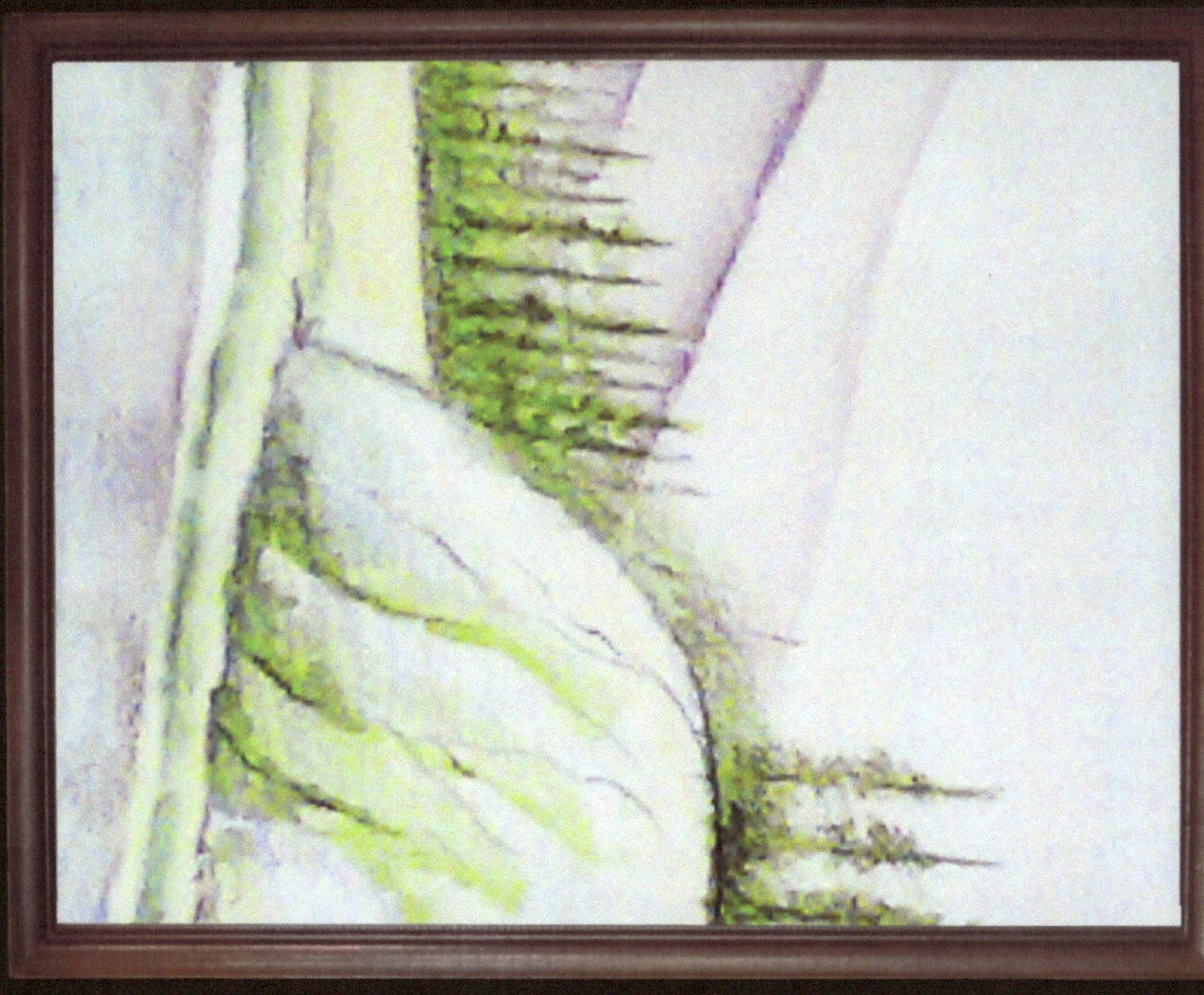

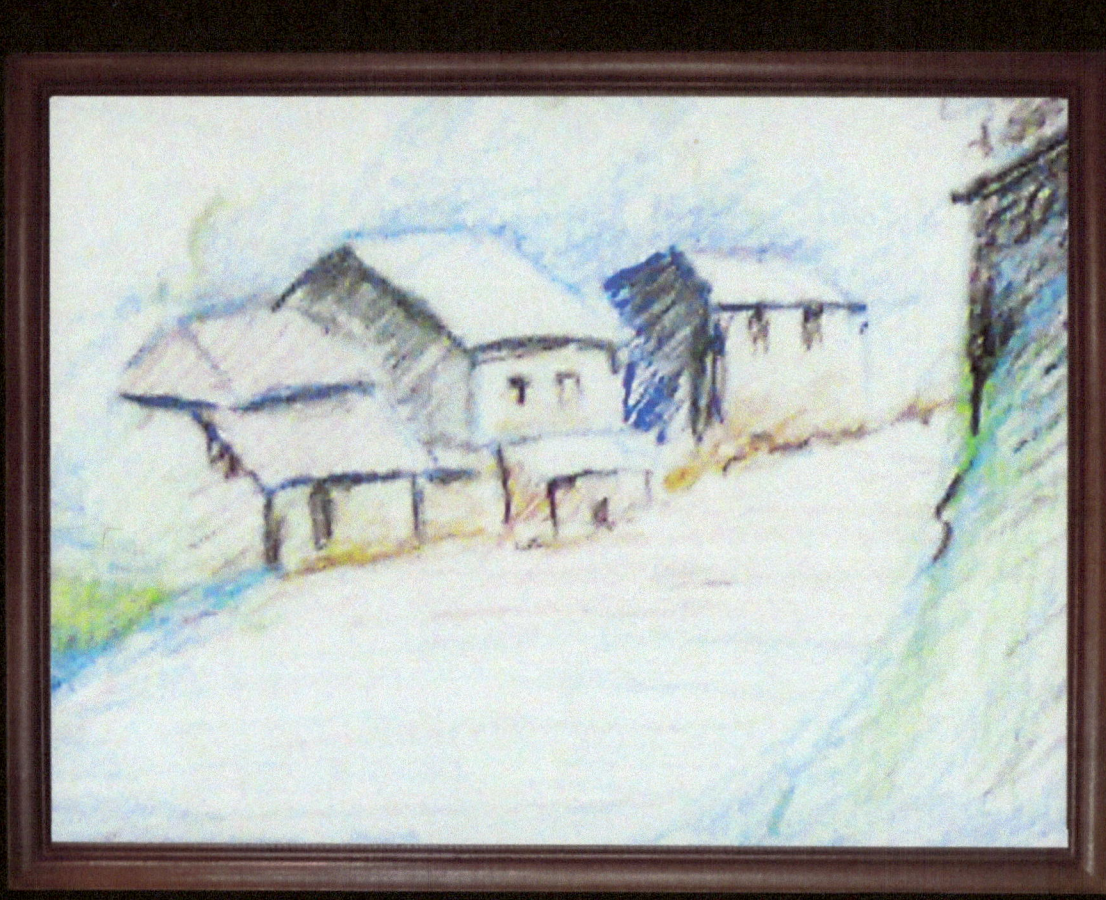

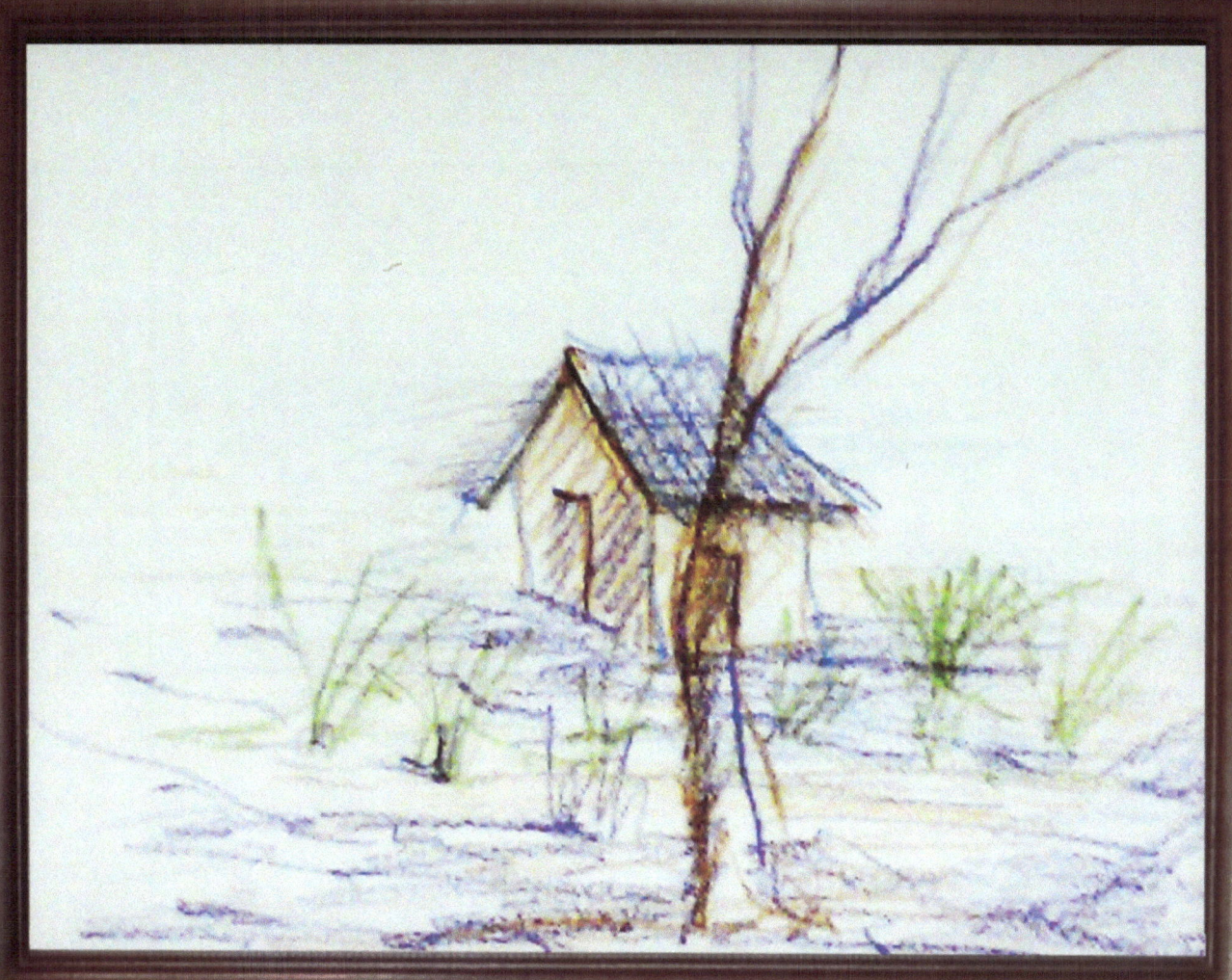

THE END

www.ingramcontent.com/pod-product-compliance
Lightning Source LLC
Chambersburg PA
CBHW050356180526
45159CB00005B/2044